DON'T GO THERE!

DON'T GO THERE!

*1001 Rude Things People Have Said
About Places in Britain & Ireland*

Colin Plinth

Weidenfeld & Nicolson
LONDON

First published in Great Britain in 2007
by Weidenfeld & Nicolson

10 9 8 7 6 5 4 3 2 1

A CIP catalogue record for this book
is available from the British Library.

ISBN-13 978 0 297 85348 0

Typeset by Goldust Design
Printed in Great Britain by Clays Ltd, St Ives plc

Weidenfeld & Nicolson

The Orion Publishing Group Ltd
Orion House
5 Upper Saint Martin's Lane
London, WC2H 9EA
www.orionbooks.co.uk

The Orion Publishing Group's policy is to use papers that are natural,
renewable and recyclable products and made from wood grown in
sustainable forests. The logging and manufacturing processes are expected
to conform to the environmental regulations of the country of origin.

Aberdeen

'God-forsaken wind-whipped streets'

The god-forsaken wind-whipped streets around Aberdeen's fish market … wee women with haggis-legs and fish-heads manked in their hair …
Euan Ferguson, *Observer*, 18 December 2005

Ferguson, a native of Edinburgh, *really* doesn't like Aberdeen, having earlier described it (in 2002) as
The armpit of these islands, moist with a cold drizzle of greed, cant and mendacity.

In the same month, Martin Amis caused outrage in Scotland's third city when he described it as
The epicentre of gloom
and
… one of the darkest places imaginable, like Iceland …

Christopher Brookmyre, Glaswegian proponent of 'Tartan Noir', caused similar distress when he described Aberdonians as

Greedy, humourless, ungrateful, conceited and whingeing
in his 2001 novel *A Big Boy Did It and Ran Away*.

But, as *Scotland on Sunday* pointed out at the time, these were just the latest in a long line of critics …

I walked for nearly three hours up streets and down and I couldn't find anything remotely adorable about Aberdeen … It wasn't that there was anything *wrong* with Aberdeen exactly, more that it suffered from a surfeit of innocuousness.
Bill Bryson, *Notes from a Small Island* (1995)

I came to hate Aberdeen more than any other place I saw. Yes, yes, the streets were clean; but it was an awful city … It was only in Aberdeen that I saw kilts and eightsome reels and the sort of tartan tightfist-edness that made me think of the average Aberdonian as a person who would gladly pick a halfpenny out of a dunghill with his teeth.
Paul Theroux, *The Kingdom by the Sea* (1983)

**Bleakness, not meanness or jollity, is the keynote to
Aberdonian character … For anyone passing their
nights and days in the Silver City by the Sea … it is
comparable to passing one's existence in a refrigerator.**
Lewis Grassic Gibbon, *Scottish Scene, or the Intelligent
Man's Guide to Albyn*, 'Aberdeen' (1934)

If you can't laugh with them …

When the Scottish comedian Sir Harry Lauder
was playing a theatre in Aberdeenshire, he was
distressed at the unresponsiveness of the audience. However, his anxiety was relieved when he
overheard a member of the audience say to his
companion after the show:

**Fit a gran comic. It took me aa ma time nae
to lach.**
[What a grand comic. It took me all my time not
to laugh.]

Just as the English make jokes about the meanness of Scotsmen, so the rest of Scotland makes jokes about the meanness of Aberdonians. The genre goes back many decades, as these few examples from the 1920s testify:

It's on record that an Aberdonian once gave a waiter a tip – but the horse came last.

A drouthy Aberdonian desirous of quenching his thirst found that he only had sixpence all told, whereas ninepence was necessary. He solved the problem by pawning the sixpence for fivepence and selling the pawn ticket for fourpence. He thus obtained ninepence and got his pint of beer.

It was at another bar that another son of the Granite City lingered a long time while examining his change. 'Is it no' right?' asked the barmaid. 'Aye,' the man replied. 'Just.'

Aberdeen FC

I've been a Hearts fan all of my life
And many a sight I've seen
But the northern lights of Aberdeen
Mean sweet fuck all to me!
Chant sung by Hearts fans

Sheepshagging bastards!
You're only sheepshagging bastards!
Sheepshagging bastards!
You're only sheepshagging bastards!
Chant sung by Glasgow Rangers fans

Aberystwyth

The unpronounceable

Two American tourists are driving round Wales, and eventually arrive in Aberystwyth. They are perplexed as to how to say the name on the signposts, so when they stop for a meal they walk up to the counter of the fast-food establishment and say, 'Can you settle an argument for us, please? Can you say the name of this place very slowly?'

'Certainly, sir. Burrrrr-gerrrrr Kiiiiiing.'

Visitors to the www.nowhere.co.uk website have logged a number of complaints about Aberystwyth:

- Local beach made of dirt.
- Nothing to do but sit around and drink.
- Welsh Nats. Best not to say anything to these people. These people are mad. You have an English accent? Don't get into a political discussion with these types – the first disagreement and they'll want a fight!
- Rain, wind – being in Wales, they can't really be avoided though.

Aran Islands

**Rumour has it that the Aran Islands are rolled
up when the tourist season ends and towed into
Galway, where workmen chip away at the rocks
to make them look a bit more rugged.**
Terry Eagleton, *The Truth About the Irish* (2001)

The Aran Islands were, of course, the inspiration for
Craggy Island, Father Ted's remote and backward parish.
The islanders are so proud of this fact that war broke
out in 2007 between two of the islands, Inis Mór and
Inis Oírr, as to which was **the *real* Craggy Island**.

Arbroath
'The clock stopped about 1950'

**The clock stopped about 1950. Everybody on the
streets looks about 60 and they all wear the same
sorts of clothes.**
Belinda Rathbone, *The Guynd: A Scottish Journal* (2006)

Aylesbury

A euphemism for fuck

In 20th-century rhyming slang *Aylesbury duck*, or simply *Aylesbury*, was used as a euphemistic substitute for *fuck* in such phrases as 'not give an Aylesbury'. Hence also Aylesbury'ed (as in 'I'm absolutely Aylesbury'ed after climbing all those stairs').
John Ayto and Ian Crofton, *Brewer's Britain and Ireland* (2005)

Balham

'Bal-ham – Gateway to the South'

So satirized by Frank Muir and Denis Norden:
Broad-bosomed, bold, becalmed, benign
Lies Balham, foursquare on the Northern Line;
Matched by no marvel save in Eastern scene,
A rose-red city half as gold as green.
Frank Muir and Denis Norden, 'Bal-ham – Gateway to the South' (1958)

Barnsley

… a town called Black Barnsley, eminent still for the working of iron and steel; and indeed the very town looks as black and smoky as if they were all smiths that lived in it; though it is not, I suppose, called Black Barnsley on that account, but for the black hue or colour of the moors, which, being covered in heath … look all black …
Daniel Defoe, *A Tour Through the Whole Island of Great Britain* (1724–6)

Two and a half centuries later Barnsley would of course provide a sufficiently grim backdrop for Ken Loach's film *Kes*.

Basildon
'Fifty years of inbreeding'

Basildon suffers from fifty years of inbreeding (in addition to the hundreds of years of keeping it in

the family practised by the original East-End
overspill who originally populated this urban
paradise). Yes, this is where even people from
Lewisham are classed as 'posh-talking bastards'
and left with permanent imprints of Reebok
trainers on their skulls.

'alexexanderdelarge', chavtowns.co.uk, December 2005

Q. What do you call an Essex girl with an IQ of 150?
A. Basildon.

People in Basildon are nearly all very friendly, good,
hardworking people. My family included. Despite
being the butt of many jokes, Basildon folk are
resilient and clever. In fact Basildon is such a good
place that I moved to London four years ago.

www.knowhere.co.uk

The same contributor-authored website lists among
the 'Worst Things' about Basildon:

Most of the population in Basildon!! Most either
wanna be Ali G or had to leave school coz they thought
a Mars bar wrapper could be used as a condom.

Basingstoke

'Better than Milton Keynes'

**Don't take the piss, it's better than Milton Keynes …
just.**
Motto of the blog Basingstokelife

The town's Soviet-style blocks have also earned it the
name Basingrad (on the model of Stalingrad). But it
is more famously nicknamed Boringstoke. The very
sound of the word 'Basingstoke' was enough to bring
Mad Margaret in Gilbert and Sullivan's *Ruddigore*
back to her senses. One former resident has observed:
**When you're bored or depressed, you can cheer
yourself up by saying, 'Well, at least I don't live in
Basingstoke any more.'**

Despite a reputation for dullness, Basingstoke makes
a number of literary appearances. Shakespeare made
a sly dig at the place in *Henry IV, Part 2* (II.i):
Lord Chief Justice: Where lay the King last night?
Gower: At Basingstoke, my Lord.
Falstaff: I hope, my Lord, all's well …

Thomas Hardy depicted Basingstoke as Stoke Barehills:
**It stands with its gaunt, unattractive, ancient
church, and its new red brick suburb, amid the
open, chalk-soiled cornlands … The most familiar
object in Stoke Barehills nowadays is its cemetery …**
Jude the Obscure (1894–5)

Basingstoke has also been dubbed **Doughnut City**,
for the number of roundabouts littering the place
(one even gets a mention in *The Hitch-Hiker's Guide
to the Galaxy*). According to the website
www.basingstoke.me.uk:
**The body of a Basingstoker who died in the middle
of the massive 'Town Centre West' roundabout
wasn't found for four days. Another Basingstoker
'lost' several hours whilst crossing this roundabout
and claimed to have been abducted by aliens.**

'I want to go back to Basingstoke.'
'But nobody wants to go back to Basingstoke.'
Dialogue from Simon Shore's film *Get Real* (1998)

Bath

Do you know, I get so immoderately sick of Bath!
Your brother and I were agreeing this morning that,
though it is vastly well to be here for a few weeks, we
would not live here for millions.
Isabella Thorpe in Jane Austen's *Northanger Abbey*
(1818)

Bedford
'Dullsville'

I know, I know: it sounds like dullsville. Goodness,
it's even got 'bed' in its name – why not go the whole
hog and call it Zzzzzford? … Every evening it's
pumped full of returning commuters whose wildest
aspirations extend to the crazy heights of an early
night, with the 2.4 kids staying over at Nan's.
Tom Dyckhoff, *Guardian*, 12 November 2005

Belfast

'As uncivilized as ever'

Belfast … as uncivilized as ever – savage black mothers in houses of dark red brick, friendly manufacturers too drunk to entertain you when you arrive. It amuses me till I get tired.
E.M. Forster, letter to T.E. Lawrence, 3 May 1928

A fine place with a rough people.
Charles Dickens, letter to his sister-in-law, 1858

[In Belfast] There is no aristocracy – no culture – no grace – no leisure worthy of the name. It all boils down to mixed grills, double whiskies, dividends, movies, and these strolling, homeless, hate-driven poor.
Sean O'Faolain, *Irish Journey* (1941)

Berkshire

All Berkshire women are very silly. I don't know why women in Berkshire are more silly than anywhere else.
Mr Justice Claude Duveen, Reading County Court, July 1972.

Incidentally, the slang term *berk* is from *Berkshire Hunt*, rhyming slang for *cunt*.

Berwick-upon-Tweed

It is old, decayed, and neither populous nor rich.
Daniel Defoe, *A Tour Through the Whole Island of Great Britain* (1724–6)

There is a famous old rhyme recited by Berwickers themselves:
Berwick is an ancient town,
A church without a steeple,

A pretty girl at every door
And very generous people.

To which Robert Burns responded with:
A bridge without a middle arch,
A church without a steeple,
A midden heap in every street
And damned conceited people.

Bexhill-on-Sea

Appropriate enough for the jewel in the crown of the Costa Geriatrica, Bexhill has a street named Terminus Avenue. But it also has a thriving youth community …

Looking out of the train at the station before disembarking in this lively seaside resort, one can see signs that this is an up-and-coming residence for the discerning chav. A station that once was a boring, old, busy listed building now clearly shows its potential for excitement with 21st-century modernization

techniques in use, such as broken windows, graffiti, discarded cigarette packets, Special Brew cans and pools of vomit. These examples of the expanding contemporary youth culture's diverse and engaging hobbies and interests are proof that Bexhill would deserve the title of 'Capital of Culture for the Bexhill-on-Sea Region' should it ever be awarded.

'JoeViterbo', chavtowns.co.uk

Billericay

Home of Ian Dury's 'Billericay Dickie', prototypical Essex Man:

Good evening! I'm from Essex, in case you
*   couldn't tell,*
My given name is Dickie, I come from Billericay,
And I'm doin' very well.
'ad a love affair with Nina
In the back of my Cortina,
A seasoned-up hyena
Could not've been more obscener.

Birmingham

'Not a place to promise much'

They came from Birmingham, which is not a place to promise much, you know ... One has not great hopes from Birmingham. I always say there is something direful in the sound.
Mrs Elton in Jane Austen's *Emma* (1816)

The longest chapter in Deuteronomy has not curses enough for an Anti-Bromingham.
John Dryden, 'To the Reader' (1681)

It's a disgusting town with villas and slums and ready made clothes shops and Chambers of Commerce.
Evelyn Waugh, diary, 1925

An unspeakable excrescence of a city ... as if God had unwisely partaken the night before of a divine Vindaloo of horrific pungency, and promptly evacuated his bowels over the West Midlands the next morning. The people pallid, corpse-like, moronic;

the buildings so ugly as to induce a sense of nausea in the hapless onlooker.

In Jonathan Coe's novel *The Closed Circle* (2004) the character of Benjamin Trotter quotes the opinion of Birmingham of the poet Francis Piper.

Birmingham: It's Not Shit

This admirable website is to be found at www.birminghamitsnotshit.co.uk. Among the jewels to be found therein is the following:

People underestimate Birmingham as a holiday destination, those looking for 'sex, sand and surf' especially – but anyone who's seen the sunrise over Acocks Green on bin day can understand that Birmingham is God's chosen holiday destination.

The writer claims to have found a palm-lined

beach under Spaghetti Junction, and concludes:
**I would fully recommend a trip to this fine
beach as part of a longer break in the
Brummagem area. Maybe you could combine it
with a visit to the One Stop Shopping centre, a
charming local bazaar selling Midlands arte-
facts like '3 lighters for a quid'.**

In 2005 visitors to the site voted Babu the Red
Panda as Brummie of the Year. With 231 votes he
was way ahead of contenders such as Bill Oddie
(43 votes) and Noddy Holder (49 votes).

One visitor to the site offered:
**Birmingham has three syllables in it, one more
than London and Paris and New York and two
more than Hull. That means that it is better.**

Hmm.

The site also quotes from an early 1980s British

travelogue film, presented by Telly ('Kojak')
Savalas, who concludes:
**You feel as if you've been projected into the 21st
century. Yes, it's my kinda town. So long,
Birmingham. Here's looking at ya.**

Hmmmmmmm.

The Birmingham accent is frequently voted the least
pleasant in the UK, while, in 2005, *Reader's Digest*
magazine conducted a survey that established that
Brummies are the least courteous people in the
country. Two years later the *Sun* was reporting on a
survey that measured the circumference of people's
mouths in various parts of Britain, and concluded:
Brummie gobs are biggest.

Birmingham City FC

'You lose some, you draw some.'
Jasper Carrott in 1979

Birmingham City,
Birmingham City,
One hundred years
And won fuck all,
Birmingham City.
Chant sung by Aston Villa fans

Blackburn

'So poor and ugly'

Blackburn is so poor and ugly. I couldn't bear to live there one more day ... You can't do that to your family.
Richard Witschge, the Dutch footballer, on his decision to leave Blackburn Rovers, 1996

It always seems to be pitch-dark by 3.30 p.m. in Blackburn. There is no language school, nor is there a fitness centre. And if you want to go shopping, there is nothing to buy. When I see how people live up here, I realize how lucky I am.
Stephane Henchoz, the Swiss footballer, who signed with Blackburn Rovers in 1997

Blackpool

'Kinda sleazy'

Bill Clinton, quoted in the *Guardian*, 21 September 2005

The reason the sea goes so far out in Blackpool is that it can't face coming back in.
Old comedians' joke

Blackpool was real clutter – the buildings that were not only ugly but also foolish and flimsy, the vacationers sitting under a dark sky with their shirts off, sleeping with their mouths open, emitting hog whimpers. They were waiting for the sun to shine, but the forecast was rain for the next five months … Blackpool was perfectly reflected in the swollen guts and unhealthy fat of its beer-guzzling visitors – eight million in the summer, when Lancashire closed to come here and belch.

Paul Theroux, *The Kingdom by the Sea* (1983)

Blackpool is ugly, dirty and a long way from anywhere … its sea is an open toilet, and its attractions nearly all cheap, provincial and dire.

Bill Bryson, *Notes from a Small Island* (1995)

As for the famous Blackpool Illuminations:
Blackpool Illuminations are essentially a very long, well-lit traffic jam … The Lights were always switched on by a celebrity – in my memory, it is a perpetual rotation of Status Quo and Judith Chalmers, and the display would boast lights in the shape of My Little Pony, or Aladdin, or the cast of *Coronation Street*. The consistent theme, however, was that they were rubbish.

Laura Barton, *Guardian*, 22 June 2006

Blackpool is less Cool Britannia than Gruel
Britannia. It is 1960s Britain minus the rock'n'roll.
Sunday Times, 10 October 1999

This is a sad place that has lost its heart … Yet visitors seem happy as they stagger from one drinking
place to another picking a way round pools of urine
and vomit that appear on the streets after dark.
Adrian Saunders, Liberal Democrat MP for Torbay,
on his party conference blog, September 2005. It was
the first time the Lib Dems had held their annual
conference in Blackpool for fifteen years.

Bodmin

Placed on the edge of a moor, Bodmin has the
distinction of being the single most miserable place
in all of Cornwall. This tiny town nestles in a valley
and is home to a large mental institution and an old
prison famous for the highest prison wall ever built.
It also has some of the ugliest council housing seen

anywhere in the world. Someone in town planning really hates Bodmin.
'neo111', chavtowns.co.uk, October 2005

Bognor Regis
'Bugger Bognor'

George V, on his deathbed, when someone suggested he would soon be convalescing in the Sussex resort. Possibly apocryphal.

Bournemouth

Known both for its decaying geriatrics – for whom it is 'the Bourne from which no traveller returns' (to mangle *Hamlet*) – and for its noisy, dance- and drug-crazed youth – for whom it is … **Bo-Mo**.

In 1805, before the town itself was built, Edward

Brayley wrote of the locality:

The greatest part of this most dreary waste, serving only in the summer to support a few ordinary sheep and cattle, and to supply the neighbouring villages with firing.

In *The Dictionary of National Celebrity* (H. Eyre & W. Donaldson, 2005) Bournemouth is defined as:

The preferred retirement locale for D-list celebrities … On the award-winning beach, large corseted women tuck their skirts into their pink ballooning knickers and wade squealing into the sea. On the promenade, old men in deckchairs pass the day in thin continuous dreaming. Further inland, a fishy aroma of cod and chips, of dead crabs in buckets under boarding-house beds, hangs in the air. Rough local girls smelling like low tide on the Dogger Bank are turned away from discos by representatives of the Russian Mafia. Later, in a bus shelter, they receive a sexual hammering from visiting roustabouts. Cannon and Ball and Anita Harris star in the summer show at the Pavilion Theatre. Celebrated residents: Max Bygraves, Matthew Kelly,

Archie Andrews, 'Whispering' Ted Lowe ('The Voice of Snooker'), Ray Allen and Lord Charles.

In its issue of 2 June 2003 the *Rockall Times*, the online satirical newspaper, offered advice on domestic holiday destinations to replace foreign spots rendered too dangerous by terrorism:

Foreign destination: Morocco

Why can't you go there? With al-Qaeda on the warpath the average Westerner's life expectancy is about 30 minutes. Two hookah pipes and you fall to pieces.

UK replacement: Bournemouth.

How so? Similar mix of sun, sand and young boys available for rent.

Bradford

'Eeeh bah gum, Bradford's glum'

Headline in the *Independent on Sunday*, 28 November 1999

Every other factory town in England is a paradise compared to this hole. In Manchester the air lies like lead upon you; in Birmingham it's as if you're sitting with your nose in a stove; in Leeds you splutter with the filth as if you had swallowed a pound of Cayenne pepper – but you can put up with all this. In Bradford, however, you are lodged with the devil incarnate … If anyone wishes to feel how a sinner is tormented in Purgatory, let him travel to Bradford.
Georg Weerth (1822–56) in 1840. Weerth was a German poet with revolutionary tendencies.

Bradford's role in life is to make every place else in the world look better in comparison, and it does this very well. Nowhere on this trip would I see a city more palpably forlorn.
Bill Bryson, *Notes from a Small Island* (1992)

It is said that Bradford is 'the town that can't afford a river' as the local stream is Bradford Beck (hence 'Bradford' is rhyming slang for 'cheque').

Brecon

The most to be said of this town is … that it is very ancient.
Daniel Defoe, *A Tour Through the Whole Island of Great Britain* (1724–6).

Bridgnorth
'Bridgnorth über alles'

In 2005 wartime papers were uncovered that revealed Bridgnorth had been destined to be the Nazi HQ in Britain should the planned German invasion of 1940 have taken place. This prompted the *Sun* to give the above headline to its version of the story.

Bridlington
'Of no note'

There is nothing remarkable upon this side [of the Humber] for above thirty miles together … Bridlington or Burlington is the only place, and that is of no note …
Daniel Defoe, *A Tour Through the Whole Island of Great Britain* (1724–6)

Some centuries later, the comedian Les Dawson observed of matinée audiences here:
You could see the dampness rising from the wet raincoats like mist on the marshes.

Brighton
'The Heaving Sodom of the South Coast'

The gay capital of England was so dubbed by Robert Hanks in the *Independent*, 4 April 2001. Hence 'Brighton Pier' is rhyming slang for 'queer'. Hence

also the chant of visiting fans when Brighton and
Hove Albion are playing (sung to the tune of
'Guantanamera'):
Down with your boyfriend,
You're going down with your boyfriend.

With a certain degree of prescience as to future
developments in linguistic usage and sexual mores,
Thackeray described Brighton in *Vanity Fair*
(1847–8) as:
Brisk, gay and gaudy, like a harlequin's jacket.

'Twas not always thus. In the 18th century, before the
Prince Regent made the place *the* place to be seen,
Dr Johnson pronounced Brighton:
Dull.
His friend Hester Piozzi reported his opinion of the
place and its surroundings thus:
**It was a country so truly desolate (he said), that if
one had a mind to hang one's self for desperation at
being obliged to live there, it would be difficult to
find a tree on which to fasten the rope.**

What's Brighton, when to thee compared? poor thing,
Whose barren hills in mist for ever weep.
John Wolcot (1738–1819), 'The Praise of Margate'

But once the Prince Regent got there, things livened
up no end:
Here I am once more in this scene of dissipation and
vice, and I begin already to find my morals corrupted.
Jane Austen, letter to Cassandra Austen, 1796

Miss Austen *really* didn't like the place:
I assure you that I dread the idea of going to
Brighton as much as you do, but I am not without
hopes that something may happen to prevent it.
Jane Austen, letter to Cassandra Austen, 8 January 1799

Brighton's reputation for 'dissipation and vice' gradu-
ally degenerated into seediness, for it was to Brighton
hotels, prior to the reform of the divorce laws in the
1960s, that gentlemen took actresses with the express
purpose of being 'surprised' *in flagrante* by paid
witnesses, so providing the necessary evidence of
adultery. Hence Keith Waterhouse's comment:

Brighton has the perennial air of being in a position to help the police with their inquiries.
Quoted in the *Observer*, 28 April 1991

Bristol

'The arsehole of the world'

I remember with Villa when we played Bristol Rovers at Twerton Park. I kept saying to the boys: 'You're going to the arsehole of the world. Think of the worst you can and it's worse than that.'
Ron Atkinson

The natives speak 'Bristle' or 'Brizzle', which, with its rolling Rs, is dubbed by outsiders 'farmer speak'. Another quaint characteristic of Bristle is the addition of a terminal L to words ending in a vowel – hence, not only Bristol itself (originally Brycgstow), but also 'ideal' (for 'idea'), 'American' (for 'America') and 'diarrheawl' (for 'diarrhoea'). Conversely, some words ordinarily pronounced with a terminal L are, in Bristle, pronounced without: hence 'Pot Nuda' (for 'Pot Noodle').

In the 19th century Bristolians were known as Bristol Hogs, while the term Bristol Man denoted a rogue or villain. And of course 'Bristols' for 'breasts' derives from the rhyming slang 'Bristol City' = 'titty'.

Rovers and City

Q. Why do Bristol City carry lighters around with them?
A. Because they lose all their matches.

Two men are fishing on a riverbank in a remote area of Somerset on a Saturday afternoon miles away from a radio or TV. Suddenly one man turns to the other and says, 'Bristol Rovers have lost again.' The other man is astonished and says, 'How on earth do you know that?' The other man replies, 'It's quarter to five.'

Brixton

So well known for its upheavals that '**Brixton riot**' has become rhyming slang for 'diet'.

Budleigh Salterton

Where everything is forbidden

I have rarely seen so many prohibitory notices on one stretch of railings – do not feed the seagulls, do not ride your bike, do not park here, do not remove natural material from the beach, no dogs. We noticed again that phenomenon of the English seaside: couples who drive to the front and park, gazing glumly out to sea, occasionally pecking at small packets of sandwiches. Perhaps they were afraid that by leaving the car they would risk infringing one of the many ordinances.
Simon Hoggart, *Guardian*, 2 April 2005

Burnham on Crouch

Caustic lines from Ian Dury's song 'Billericay
Dickie' reflect the town's naffly moneyed aura:
Oh golly, oh gosh, come and lie on the couch
With a nice bit of posh from Burnham on Crouch.
John Ayto and Ian Crofton, *Brewer's Britain and*
Ireland (2005)

Burnley
'Twinned with Hell'

Your town is twinned with Hell,
You're ugly and you smell.
Chant sung by fans of Blackburn Rovers

A nice guy from Burnley, which is not oxymoronic
despite what you Tykes might think.
Jim Perrin, in *Climber* magazine, February 2006

Comparisons are Odious

These ones are from the Alternative Blackpool website:

- **Half a million eggs and two million rashers of bacon are eaten for breakfast in Blackpool each day. (Comparison with Burnley: In Burnley the main breakfast dish of the day is the dead cats which they find in dustbins.)**
- **Nearly 19,000 deck chairs are hired out in Blackpool each day. (Comparison with Burnley: Chairs are unknown in Burnley as its inhabitants are still at the squatting stage of evolution.)**
- **The number of hot dogs eaten in Blackpool each day would stretch forty-seven and a half miles if laid end to end. (Comparison with Burnley: A hot dog is a type of sausage, not a barbequed canine as it is in Burnley.)**

The town of Burnley lies in a valley amidst ragged moorland, from which its inhabitants have formed an unnatural affection for sheep.
The Alternative Blackpool website

And so this is Burnley, and what have we done,
We've lost here already, would you like a cream bun.
Song favoured by despondent Burnley fans in the 1980s, sung to the tune of John Lennon's 'Happy Xmas (War is Over)'

Cambridge
'City of perspiring dreams'

So called by Frederick Raphael in *The Glittering Prizes* (1976) – playing, of course, on Oxford, the 'city of dreaming spires'.

A discouraging surfeit of concrete structures.
Bill Bryson, *Notes from a Small Island* (1995)

Oxford is on the whole more attractive than
Cambridge to the ordinary visitor; and the traveller
is therefore recommended to visit Cambridge first,
or to omit it altogether if he cannot visit both.
Karl Baedeker, *Great Britain* (1887)

For Cambridge people rarely smile,
Being urban, squat, and packed with guile.
Rupert Brooke, 'The Old Vicarage, Grantchester' (1915)

Regarding the university (dubbed by Oxonians 'the
Poly on the Fens'):
Surely it was of this place, now Cambridge but
formerly known by the name of Babylon, that the
prophet spoke when he said: 'the wild beasts of the
desert shall dwell there, and their houses shall be
full of doleful creatures, and owls shall build there,
and satyrs shall dance there'.

Thomas Gray, letter to Richard West, December 1736.
West, who was at Oxford, replied, 'Oxford, I can
assure you, has owls that match yours.'
Hail, horrors, hail! ye ever gloomy bowers,

Ye gothic fanes, and antiquated towers
Where rushy Camus' slowly winding flood
Perpetual draws his humid train of mud.
Thomas Gray, 'Hymn to Ignorance'

Men unscoured, grotesque
In character, tricked out like aged trees.
William Wordsworth on Cambridge dons in *The Prelude*. Wordsworth was at St John's College.

You can stuff your fucking boat race up your arse.
Chant sung by visiting fans at Cambridge United matches, to the tune of 'She'll Be Coming Round the Mountain'

Campbeltown
'The nearest place to nowhere'

How the locals describe the town, stuck as it is near the far-flung tip of the Kintyre peninsula.

Sunday in Campbeltown … is quite a day of gloom and penance … neither music or whistling is allowed in either the houses or streets, and the land-lady of the hotel was quite shocked at our proposing to play some sacred music on the piano … We might have expected this, as it is said that there are nearly as many places of worship as distillers in the town.
Alfred Barnard, *The Whisky Distillers of the United Kingdom* (1887)

Cardiganshire

Cardiganshire … is the richest county I ever knew, and the one which contains the fewest clever or ingenious people.
Lewis Morris, letter to William Morris, 11 February 1742

Cardis (as the natives are known) are popularly reputed to be clannish, parsimonious and excessively thrifty. Thus, among Welsh people, 'an old Cardi' denotes one reluctant to pay for his round of drinks.

There is a saying:

Cardiganshire is the land where men flourish and prosper even when the crows are starving to death.

There also many jokes on this theme:

I called in at this farm in Cardiganshire and the farmer was stripping the wallpaper. 'Decorating, Dai?' I asked. 'No,' said the farmer, 'moving house.'

Some say the traditional Cardi has been superseded by the Credit Cardi.

Cardiff

An atomic bomb went off in Cardiff and caused seven pounds worth of damage.
Joke told by Stephen Fry on his TV quiz show *QI*, 30 September 2005

Q. What's a sheep tied to a lamp post?
A. A leisure centre in Cardiff.
Joke told on the same show

Where are we? It's not Cardiff again, is it?
Frequent line in the 2005 series of *Dr Who*, much of which was filmed in Cardiff

Always shit on the Welsh side of the bridge.
Chant sung by Bristol City and Bristol Rovers fans to the tune of Monty Python's 'Always Look on the Bright Side of Life'. Cardiff fans return the compliment, substituting 'English' for 'Welsh'.

'We hate Cardiff, we hate Cardiff, we hate Cardiff, we hate Cardiff!' I yell without concession. There is no muttering that despite our general dislike of the capital city we appreciate its superior shopping facilities, that the riverside development is a vital lifeline for Welsh industry and that, in nearly every way, Cardiff is the cultural hub of Wales. But I digress. 'We hate Cardiff, we hate Cardiff, we hate Cardiff, we hate Cardiff!'
'spack', 'And it's Swansea City, Swansea City FC …', www.abctales.com

Carlisle

'Small town in Scotland'

Small town in Scotland,
You're just a small town in Scotland.
Chant sung by rival football fans to the tune of
'Guantanamera', mocking the English city's close
proximity to the Scottish Border.

During the First World War the government took
control of all the pubs and the brewery in Carlisle, as
the local munitions workers were perennially pissed.
Further misfortunes hit the city with the disastrous
floods of January 2005 (not to mention the poor
performance of the local football team). Many locals
blamed the newly commissioned Millennium Stone
engraved with the words of a curse issued against this
'lawless place' by Gavin Dunbar, Archbishop of
Glasgow, in 1525, in an effort to stem cross-border
raiding. The 1,000-word curse begins:
**I curse their head and all the hairs of their head; I
curse their face, their brain, their mouth, their nose,
their tongue, their teeth, their forehead, their**

shoulders, their breast, their heart, their stomach, their back, their womb, their arms, their legs, their hands, their feet, and every part of their body, from the top of their head to the soles of their feet, before and behind, within and without.

I could have signed for Newcastle when I was seventeen, but I decided I would be better off at Carlisle. I'd had a drink that night.
Footballer Peter Beardsley reminisces, 1994

Catford

Spike Milligan, who was brought up in the area, is reported to have exclaimed:
Christ! I must be bored. I just thought of Catford.

Chalfont St Giles

Rhyming slang for 'piles' (as in haemorrhoids).

Chatham

'A well-packed dustbin'

I have never revisited Chatham; the impression it
has left on me is one of squalid compression, unlit
by any gleam of maturer charity ... Since the whole
wide county of Kent was made up ... for the gentle-
folk, the surplus of population, all who were not
good tenants nor good labourers, Church of
England, submissive and respectful, were necessarily
thrust out of sight, to fester as they might in this
place that had the colours and even the smells of a
well-packed dustbin, They should be grateful even
for that; that, one felt, was the theory of it all.
H.G. Wells, *Tono-Bungay* (1909)

Forming, along with Gillingham and Rochester, the
Axis of Banality that is the Medway Towns,
Chatham is celebrated locally for the particularly
high quality of its young ladies ... southern
England's best-kept secret.
www.theregister.co.uk. The 'young ladies' in question
are, of course, the famous Chatham Girls, as renowned

for their decorousness and gentility as their more famous Essex cousins.

Chelmsford

If any one were to ask me what in my opinion was the dullest and most stupid spot on the face of the Earth, I should decidedly say Chelmsford.
Charles Dickens, letter, 1835

Chelsea

The nobs of Chelsea, who insist on taking Piers and Penelope the few hundred yards to school in their Chelsea tractors (4x4 gas guzzlers with bull bars and Alice-band attitude), have been called by Mayor Ken Livingstone 'complete idiots'.

That other Chelsea institution, the Chelsea Flower

Show, has been described as:

A familiar English emulsion of staggering nastiness and winning dedication.

A.A. Gill, *The Angry Island* (2006)

Chelsea FC

Shit team in Fulham,
You're just a shit team in Fulham.
Chant sung by rival football fans. The Chelsea ground is indeed located in neighbouring Fulham.

My arms withered and my body was covered in pus-filled sores, but no matter how bad it got I consoled myself by remembering I wasn't a Chelsea fan.
Ian Holloway, manager of Queen's Park Rangers, on ITV in June 2005 on how he had got through a recent bout of illness

Cheltenham

Here lie I and my four daughters
Killed by drinking Cheltenham waters,
Had we but stuck to Epsom salts
We wouldn't have been in these here vaults.
Anon., 'Cheltenham Waters'

… this place appears to be the residence of an assemblage of tax-eaters. These vermin shift about between London, Cheltenham, Bath, Bognor, Brighton, Tunbridge, Ramsgate, Margate, Worthing, and other spots in England.
William Cobbett, *Rural Rides* (1830)

Cheshire

Of the county's so-called Golden Triangle:
Its rise began, with respectable conformity, as southern Manchester's stockbroker belt, but in the latter part of the 20th century the soap stars and

**footballers moved in, and discreet good taste
slipped down the agenda.**
John Ayto and Ian Crofton, *Brewer's Britain and
Ireland* (2005)

**People from that provincial centre called London
always concentrate on the same side of Cheshire. It's
two-dimensional, Botoxed, blonde, oversexed and
overblown.**
Patrick O'Neill, editor of *Cheshire Life*, quoted in the
Independent on Sunday, 8 October 2006

**I have never come across people so obsessed with
money, who are so far removed from spiritual values.**
The Revd David Leaver, formerly of St Bartholomew's,
Wilmslow, quoted in the *Independent on Sunday*,
8 October 2006

Chew Valley

The Chew Valley is one of those patches of Olde England that turns me all patriotic, misty-eyed and indulgent towards morris dancers. Ahh, skittle evenings in crusty ale houses! Bearded men! Church steeples and village fetes! Then a convoy of SUVs thunders into view and spoils the whole charade.
Tom Dyckhoff, *Guardian*, 26 February 2005

Chichester

I cannot say much for the city of Chichester, in which, if six or seven good families were removed, there would not be much conversation, except what is to be found among the canons, and dignitaries of the cathedral.
Daniel Defoe, *A Tour Through the Whole Island of Great Britain* (1726)

Also known as Shitchester, it is known as a 'little'

city and it is 'little' in every sense, from its size to the tiny minds of its inhabitants. The place is full of arrogant, ignorant, thick ex-public school yobs who throw their weight about, hit people and patronize/ talk down to anyone they meet … If you want to enjoy life and are a decent person, avoid this nasty, unfriendly, spiteful little dump like the plague. Don't even visit it. Just leave the nasty, insular, malicious little Tory-voting wankers who live there to stew in their own crap.

'snobbychavhater', chavtowns.co.uk, December 2005

Colchester

In George Orwell's futuristic novel *1984* an atomic bomb is dropped on Colchester.

Intriguingly, these days Colchester's official tourism website throws out the following challenge:
The town dares you to embrace and enjoy it.
(Like an Essex girl, one supposes.)

Congleton
'Bear Town'

In the 16th and 17th centuries Congleton was a noted centre of bear-baiting. Tradition has it that at some time in the 16th century the town bear died just before the annual wakes week. Money intended to buy a Bible was diverted to the purchase of a new bear, hence Congleton came to be called 'Bear Town' and its inhabitants Congleton Bears. In the words of an old jingle:

Congleton rare, Congleton rare,
Sold the Bible to buy a bear.

John Ayto and Ian Crofton, *Brewer's Britain and Ireland* (2005)

Cork

Until the 18th century the area occupied by the city was intersected by channels of water:

We have often heard Cork called the Venice of Ireland,

but have never heard Venice called the Cork of Italy.
Anon., quoted by John Betjeman in a letter to
Michael Rose (25 September 1955)

**I feel at times as if I was among a people as mysteri-
ous as the Chinese, a people who have taken hold
of the English language and moulded it to their
cross-purposes.**
Conor Cruise O'Brien, comment on Cork, 1994

Beyond the city, far to the west, lies … West Cork:
**West Cork, the region where belief in the impossible
is strongest.**
www.peoplesrepublicofcork.com, 19 January 2006,
referring to the moving statue of Ballinspittle, a
Marian miracle of 1985

**West Cork … Today, it's a glamorous destination, a
haven for upmarket tourists, English expats, and
Dutch cannabis importers, but in the 1950s and
1960s it was the arse end of the back of beyond,
and that may be talking it up.**
Pete McCarthy, *McCarthy's Bar* (2000)

Cornwall

In Cornwall it's Saturday before you realize it's Thursday.
Wilfred Pickles (1904–78)

The Cotswolds

It's a spiritually and practically barren landscape, like a plastic fruit bowl only there for the decoration, to be seen from a distance.
A.A. Gill, *The Angry Island* (2006)

Coventry
'Ghost Town'

So dubbed by the Specials in their single of that name, released in 1981.

Q. What's the difference between Coventry City and
the Bermuda Triangle?
A. The Bermuda Triangle has three points.

Coventry … still mostly minging, no matter how
much cosmetic surgery they give it.
Tom Dyckhoff, *Guardian*, 11 March 2006

Cowes

Q. What's brown and steaming and comes out
of Cowes?
A: The Isle of Wight ferry.

Crewe

Stay on the train

Crewe is most famous as a rail junction:
If you're on a train the best part of the journey is

when you pass through Crewe. Why? Because you've not got off there.

'KeepCheshireClean', chavtowns.co.uk, September 2005

Crianlarich

The most signposted nowhere on the planet.
Jim Crumley, *Gulfs of Blue Air: A Highland Journey* (1997)

Crossmaglen

Once apparently a hotbed of deceit and intemperance:
I was a bold teetotaller for nine long years or more,
The neighbours all respected me, and decent clothes
   I wore.
My parents they were fond of me, 'till one unlucky
   day,
Just like a child, I was beguiled by whiskey in me tay.

*It wasn't the lads from Shercock, nor the boys from
  Ballybay,*
*But the dalin' men from Crossmaglen put whiskey
  in me tay.*
Traditional song

Croydon

**Croydon is a good market-town; but is, by the
funds, swelled out into a wen.**
William Cobbett, *Rural Rides* (1830)

**Croydon … grim bastions of dull concrete, stained
with traffic fumes and bird crap that should have
been demolished years ago; the same old shops all
over again: M&S, Boots, WH Smith, Next,
Superdrug, Carphone bloody Warehouse …**
'Weird Croydon', www.strangeplace.org

**I just remember being here once and I asked someone,
'Croydon must have been very badly bombed in the**

war?' He surprisingly said, 'No, it wasn't.'
Graham Norton, recalling a visit in the early 1990s

Croydon is regarded by some as the acme of chav-
dom, hence the expression 'Croydon facelift' for a
style favoured by chavettes all over the country, in
which the hair is scraped back so tightly into a pony-
tail that it pulls back the skin on the wearer's
cheekbones.

Cumbernauld
'Noddytown'

So nicknamed by Glasgwegians because, as a New
Town, it is not a 'real' town, and also partly as a play
on the last syllable 'nauld'.

Cumbernauld – described as 'Scotland's answer to
Kabul' – was named 'Scotland's most dismal town' in
the 2001 Carbuncle Awards. A native was quoted in
the *Guardian* (13 December 2005) as saying:

At least it's the ugliest place in the country. It would be so much worse to be the second ugliest.

In 2005 the town's shopping centre was voted Britain's most hated building in a survey for the Channel 4 programme *Demolition*:
As you walk through Cumbernauld shopping centre it is perfectly possible to imagine yourself in any provincial shopping mall in the country; which is just as well, because from the outside the only comparison is an eastern European sink estate … 'It's a total shit-hole,' sighs Kenny, a student. 'There would be a queue 50,000 long to light the touchpaper if they ever decided to demolish this place. You think it looks bad just now? You should see it when it's raining and the grey clouds have drawn in. It makes you suicidal just to look at it.'
Gerard Seenan, *Guardian*, 13 December 2005

Darlington

'Nothing remarkable but dirt.'

Daniel Defoe, *A Tour Through the Whole Island of Great Britain* (1724–6)

Deal

'A very pitiful town'

Samuel Pepys in 1660

During the infamous Great Storm of 1703, the town's inhabitants were too busy looting shipwrecked booty to rescue the survivors, who then perished on the Goodwin Sands. Daniel Defoe later wrote:

If I had any satire left to write,
Could I with suited spleen indite,
My verse should blast that fatal town,
And drown'd sailors' widows pull it down;
No footsteps of it should appear,

And ships no more cast anchor there.
The barbarous hated name of Deal shou'd die,
Or be a term of infamy;
And till that's done, the town will stand
A just reproach to all the land.

A most villainous place. It is full of filthy-looking people. Great desolation of abomination has been going on here … Everything seems upon the perish. I was glad to hurry along through it, and to leave its inns and public-houses to be occupied by the tarred, and trowsered, and blue-and-buff crew whose very vicinage I always detest.
William Cobbett, *Rural Rides* (1822)

Derby

'Where is Derby?'

Joan Collins, as guest quizmistress on *Have I Got News For You*, 19 December 2005

It is perhaps a reflection on the place that when Bonnie Prince Charlie and his Highland army reached Derby in 1745, they turned round and fled back to Scotland.

Q. What do you call a Derby fan with lots of girlfriends?
A. A shepherd.

Devon

'This dull Devonshire'

More discontents I never had
Since I was born, than here;
Where I have been, and still am sad
In this dull Devonshire.
Robert Herrick (1591–1674), 'Discontents in Devon'

Devonshire … is a splashy, rainy, misty … floody, muddy, slipshod County.
John Keats, letter, 1818

Diss

The meanest town in Britain?

In 2003 Diss achieved the distinction of being labelled 'the meanest town in Britain' after it was revealed that it only had £5 in its Christmas lights fund. The following year traders in Diss managed to raise £13,000.

Doncaster

Cruelty, covetousness, calculation, insensibility, and low wickedness.
Charles Dickens, in 1857, listing the qualities on display among the visitors to Doncaster in the week of the St Leger, 'a gathering of vagabonds from all parts of the racing earth'. Dickens continued:
If a boy with any good in him, but with a dawning propensity to sporting and betting, were but brought to the Doncaster races soon enough, it would cure him.

A century and a half later, Doncaster's other notable sporting venue, the ground of Doncaster Rovers, attracted this comment:

You wouldn't take the kids along for fear they might catch something.

Mark Weaver, acting manager of Doncaster Rovers, on the state of the facilities at the ground, 1998

Have you been to Donny lately? They've knocked most of it down. It looks much better.

'polko', www.drownedinsound.com, 6 May 2004

A Doncaster Rovers player is spotted by a Manchester United scout and is asked to go to Old Trafford for a trial. After impressing the coaching staff and Sir Alex Ferguson, he is invited into the manager's office and Fergie says, 'Son, I haven't seen anyone with your talent for a long time. How would you like a contract starting at £25,000 per week?' The lad replies, '£25,000 per week! I was lucky to get £250 at Doncaster!' Ferguson continues, 'Well, son, we're talking Man United here … the best team in the country. You've got to aim high and

think big! I've also arranged a house for you, a seven-bed detached in Wilmslow, set in five acres with its own pool and tennis courts.' The lad is ecstatic. 'Seven-bed detached! I've only got a council flat at Doncaster!' Ferguson continues, 'I told you, we're talking Man United here … the best team in the country. You've got to aim high and think big! I've also arranged your transport, a Jaguar XK8 for the week and a Ferrari F50 for the weekend.' The lad is on cloud nine. 'A Jag and a Ferrari! I only had a Reliant Robin at Doncaster!' Ferguson continues, 'I told you, we're talking Man United here … the best team in the country. You've got to aim high and keep thinking big! Right, I will put you on at the start of the game, but don't be surprised if I pull you off at half time.' The lad can't believe it. 'Pull me off at half time! I just got an orange at Doncaster!'

Dorking

Dorking is what farm boys do to their pigs.
Spike Greene

Dover

'Like a marine ostrich'

The little narrow, crooked town of Dover hid itself away from the beach, and ran its head into the chalk cliffs, like a marine ostrich … The air among the houses was of so strong a piscatory flavour that one might have supposed sick fish went up to be dipped in it, as sick people went down to be dipped in the sea. A little fishing was done in the port, and a quantity of strolling about by night, and looking seaward: particularly at those times when the tide made, and was near flood. Small tradesmen, who did no business whatever, sometimes unaccountably realized large fortunes, and it was remarkable that nobody in the neighbourhood could endure a lamplighter.

Charles Dickens, *A Tale of Two Cities* (1859)

The 'Welcome to Dover' sign is more an introduction to English humour than an actual greeting.
Paul Gogarty, *The Coast Road* (2004)

Dublin
'The most disagreeable place in Europe'

This town … I believe is the most disagreeable place in Europe, at least to any but those who have been accustomed to it from their youth, and in such a case I suppose a jail might be tolerable.
Jonathan Swift, letter to Knightly Chetwode, 23 November 1727

Boswell: **Should you not like to see Dublin, Sir?**
Johnson: **No, Sir! Dublin is only a worse capital.**
James Boswell, *The Life of Samuel Johnson* (1791) (conversation on 12 October 1779)

Dublin, though a place much worse than London, is not so bad as Iceland.
Samuel Johnson, quoted in a note in later editions of Boswell's *Life*

My intention was to write a chapter of the moral history of my country and I chose Dublin for the scene because that city seemed to me the centre of paralysis.
James Joyce, letter to Grant Richards, 1905

Dublin has one advantage – it is easy to get out of it.
Oliver St John Gogarty in 1937

The Irish are the niggers of Europe … An' Dubliners are the niggers of Ireland … An' the northside Dubliners are the niggers o' Dublin – Say it loud. I'm black an' I'm proud.
Roddy Doyle, *The Commitments* (1987). Doyle has also said of Dublin:
It's a big con job, we have sold the myth of Dublin as a sexy place incredibly well; because it's a dreary little dump most of the time. Try getting a pint at

one in the morning and you'll find just how raving it actually is.

If architecture is indeed a 'frozen music' (the metaphor, attributed by different sources to Goethe, Schelling and Le Corbusier), the panoramic view from the top of the chimney [of the old Jameson distillery] could be compared to an ear-grating cacophony, played by a madman. Dublin's chaotic cityscape was reminiscent of a huge sack of potatoes that had burst at the seams and was carelessly dropped onto the ground ... A depressive and largely dysfunctional metropolis, with high crime rate, all-permeating corruption, unworkable transport system and one of Europe's worst-dressed street crowds.
Vitali Vitaliev, 'Dublin', www.travelintelligence.com

A New Year resolution from www.peoplesrepublicof-cork.com, 11 January 2006:
Try to go the whole year without visiting Dublin (attending Croke Park the only exception). Nothing wins approval and respect in a Cork pub more

than being able to say, 'Yera, I wouldn't know …
sure I haven't been to Dublin in years', when somebody brings up a topic relating to the Dirty Aul
Town. You contribute enough to Dublin with your
taxes, why contribute more to their economy with
your presence? At the end of the day Dublin has
nothing for the Corkonian but a tiny zoo, a spike and
pubs that you'd have to get a bank loan out especially
to get drunk.

Dudley

**A bleak concrete wasteland inhabited by serial
murderers, masochists, occultists and freaks.**
Patrick Thomson, *Seeing the Wires* (2002). The mayor
of Dudley was outraged, declaring the author should
seek psychiatric help.

Dundee

'Unparalleled charmlessness'

A façade of unparalleled charmlessness, an absence of grace so total that it was almost a thing of wonder.
James Cameron in 1967. Paul Theroux has described the place as 'an interesting monstrosity'. During the Cold War Dundee was often used by film-makers to stand in for some drab Eastern European city.

Lewis Grassic Gibbon personified the city thus:
A frowsy fisher-wife addicted to gin and infanticide.

Alongside trials for crimes against humanity, it would be good to set up an international tribunal for crimes against towns and cities to punish those responsible for destroying their faces and souls. Dundee could be both a victim and a witness for the prosecution at such a trial.
Vitali Vitaliev, 'Dundee', www.travelintelligence.com

Dundee: Home to the World's Worst Poet

William McGonagall, who worked as a carpet weaver in the city, offered this backhanded compliment in his poem 'Bonnie Dundee' in 1878:

There's no other town I know of with you can compare
For spinning mills and lasses fair …

A few years later, however, he had had enough:

Welcome! Thrice welcome to the year 1893
For it is the year that I intend to leave Dundee
Owing to the treatment I receive
Which does my heart sadly grieve.

An odd place, like Wapping.
Charles Dickens, letter, 1858. He was in Dundee to give readings from his works, and he thought the people 'in respect of taste and intelligence, below any other of my Scotch audiences'.

[There is] a certain perverse masochism in the Dundonian … designed to keep intruders, visitors and tourists at bay.
Professor Charles McKean of Dundee University, quoted in Vitaliev, op. cit.

Q. Why is there a toll on the Tay Bridge going south from Dundee, but not on the way north to the city?
A. To make sure at least *somebody* stays in Dundee.

Dundee. Worst city on this planet. Famous for prisoners at Forfar jail preferring to stay in prison than visit it for a day-trip. Populated by subsidy junkies, tinks, soap-dodgers, coagies, etc., all financed by the charitable folk in Perth.
'A Guide to Saintee [i.e. St Johnstone, the Perth club] Terminology',
www.grange.demon.co.uk/saints/guide.htm

Dundee FC. Scumdee, the Great Unwashed, the tinks from doon the Tay.
Ibid.

Q. What's the difference between a Dundee girl and
   a walrus?
A. One's big, fat, grey and smells of fish, the other
   one's a walrus.

Eastbourne

Like Purgatory …

**Purgatory is Heaven's waiting room. Like
Eastbourne without the beach.**
Stuart Jeffries, *Guardian*, 6 October 2006

Apparently, more than 55 per cent of ASBOs in
Eastbourne are served on OAPs. But it turns out that
this is for such antisocial behaviour as blasting out
Des O'Connor at four in the morning, or, in the case
of one elderly gentleman, for sunbathing in nothing
but a see-through, heart-shaped lady's thong.

East Grinstead

'A sort of nothing town'

Funny place, East Grinstead. Nothing remarkable, on the face of it – just masses of Stockbroker Tudor mansions on the outskirts, a messily indeterminate centre, if you can call it that, and then a sprawl of smaller houses fading into industrial estates. Neither charming nor particularly ugly: just a sort of nothing town.

George Hay, 'Sleeper' (1995)

The world Scientology HQ is based in East Grinstead, which suddenly makes Bethlehem seem like Manhattan.

Marina Hyde, *Guardian*, 5 November 2005

Ecclefechan

This unfortunate, wicked little village.

Robert Burns

Edinburgh

'The Reykjavik of the South'

So dubbed by Tom Stoppard in *Jumpers* (1972),
in response to Edinburgh's preferred moniker, 'the
Athens of the North'

**A disappointed spinster, with a hare-lip and
inhibitions.**
Lewis Grassic Gibbon, personifying Edinburgh in his
essay 'Glasgow'

**Cold and grim and apparently under water for nine
months of the year.**
A.L. Kennedy, *Observer*, 25 September 2005

The bitter east, the misty summer
And grey metropolis of the North.
Alfred, Lord Tennyson, 'The Daisy'

**This city is placed in a dainty, healthful pure air,
and doubtless were a most healthful place to live in**

were not the inhabitants most sluttish, nasty and
slothful people.
Sir William Brereton, journal, 1636 (Brereton was
from Cheshire)

My curse upon your whunstane hearts,
Ye E'nbrugh gentry!
Robert Burns

Glaswegians regard Edinburgh folk as
aw fur coat an nae knickers
and have a number of pertinent sayings, for example:

**You can have more fun at a Glasgow funeral than at
an Edinburgh wedding.**

**Edinburgh! A castle, a smile and a song … One out
of three can't be bad.**

Edinburgh: City of Stinks

Edinburgh's medieval Old Town, with its narrow streets and lanes, was a famously smelly place. From the higher floors of the tall tenement buildings chambermaids would empty chamber pots onto the streets below, with a cry of 'Gardyloo'. After James Boswell and Dr Johnson visited in 1773 the former recalled:

Mr Johnson and I walked arm in arm up the High Street to my house in James Court; it was a dusky night; I could not prevent his being assailed by the evening effluvia of Edinburgh. As we marched along he grumbled in my ear 'I smell you in the dark.'

A couple of decades later, in 1798, the Reverend Sydney Smith wrote:

No smells were ever equal to Scotch smells. It is the School of Physic; walk the streets, and you would imagine that every medical man had been

administering cathartics to every man, woman and child in the town. Yet the place [Edinburgh] is uncommonly beautiful, and I am in a constant balance between admiration and trepidation:

Taste guides my eye, where e'er new beauties spread,
While prudence whispers, 'Look before you tread.'

The following century saw little improvement in conditions in Edinburgh's Old Town – as Charles Dickens described in the 1850s, recalling an earlier visit:

In the closes and wynds of that picturesque place (I am sorry to remind you what fast friends picturesqueness and typhus often are), we saw more poverty and sickness in an hour than many people would believe in, in a life. Our way lay from one to another of the most wretched dwellings, reeking with horrible odours; shut out from the sky and from the air, mere pits and dens.

Egham

Egham for me is like a comb crossed with a sponge.
Peter O'Toole

England
'Women Vomiting in the Streets'

I was amazed when I came to this country at the way the women behave. From London to Newcastle to Leeds to Manchester I saw women vomiting in the streets. It is disgusting the way they behave. In France the women will only drink a little bit – because they have to drive their husbands home.
David Ginola, quoted in the *Observer*, 4 May 2003

Plus ça change:
A population sodden with drink, steeped in vice, eaten up by every social and physical malady, these are the denizens of Darkest England amidst whom my life has been spent.

William Booth, founder of the Salvation Army,
In Darkest England, and the Way Out (1880)

God, what a hole, what witless crapulous people.
Philip Larkin, letter to Robert Conquest, 24 July 1955

Curse the blasted, jelly-boned swines, the slimy, the belly-wriggling invertebrates, the miserable sodding rotters, the flaming sods, the snivelling, dribbling, palsied, pulseless lot that make up England. They've got white of egg in their veins, and their spunk is that watery it's a marvel they can breed … Why, why, why, was I born an Englishman! – my cursed, rotten-boned, pappy-hearted countrymen, *why* was I sent to *them*?
D.H. Lawrence, letter to Edward Garnett, 3 July 1912,
after a publisher had rejected *Sons and Lovers*

There are only three things against living in Britain: the place, the climate and the people.
Jimmy Edwards

Regarding the people, Cyril Connolly described the English as:

Sheep with a nasty side.
Quoted by Gavin Ewart in *Quarto*, 1980

The English talk loudly and seem to care little for other people. This is their characteristic, and a very brutal and barbarous distinction it is.
The Reverend Sydney Smith

England has become a squalid, uncomfortable, ugly place … an intolerant, racist, homophobic, narrow-minded, authoritarian rat-hole run by vicious suburban-minded, materialistic philistines.
Hanif Kureishi in 1988, quoted in Patrick Higgins, ed., *A Queer Reader* (1993)

England's not a bad country … It's just a mean, cold, ugly, divided, tired, clapped-out, post-imperial, post-industrial slag-heap covered in polystyrene hamburger cartons.
Margaret Drabble, *A Natural Curiosity* (1989)

England is a horrible place with horrible people, horrible food, horrible climate, horrible class system, horrible cities and horrible countryside.
Stephen Pile, *Sunday Times*

Living in England, provincial England, must be like being married to a stupid but exquisitely beautiful wife.
Margaret Halsey, *With Malice Toward Some* (1938)

A soggy little island huffing and puffing to keep up with Western Europe.
John Updike, 'London Life' (1969), *Picked Up Pieces* (1976)

Racial characteristics:
Cold-blooded queers with nasty complexions and terrible teeth who once conquered half the world but still haven't figured out central heating. They warm their beers and chill their baths and boil all their food.
P.J. O'Rourke, 'Foreigners Around the World', *National Lampoon*, 1976

If an Englishman gets run down by a truck, he apologises to the truck.
Jackie Mason, American comedian, quoted in the *Independent*, 20 September 1990

The cold of the polar regions was nothing to the chill of an English bedroom.
Explorer Fridtjof Nansen, quoted in Daniele Varè, *The Laughing Diplomat* (1939)

The Englishman has all the qualities of a poker except its occasional warmth.
Daniel O'Connell

… a typical Englishman, always dull and usually violent.
Oscar Wilde, *An Ideal Husband* (1895)

The English have always been a wicked race.
Charlotte Elizabeth, duchess of Orléans, letter to her stepsister Louisa, 13 January 1718

The English, who eat their meat red and bloody, show the savagery that goes with such food.
Julien Offroy de La Mettrie (1709–51), French physician and philosopher

The English are, I think, the most obscure and barbarous people in the world.
Stendhal

In Anglo-Saxon countries men prefer the company of other men … In England 25 per cent of men are homosexual.
Edith Cresson, French prime minister, in 1991

We are all too inclined to see [England] as a produc-tion line for tattooed, alcoholic and dangerous hooligans.
Le Monde, July 1998, during the World Cup competition held in France

From every Englishman emanates a kind of gas, the deadly choke-damp of boredom.
Heinrich Heine

The English are the people of consummate cant.
Friedrich Nietzsche, *Twilight of the Idols* (1889)

Paralytic sycophants
Effete betrayers of humanity
Carrion-eating servile imitators
Arch-cowards and collaborators
Gang of women-murderers
Degenerate rabble
Parasitic traditionalists
Playboy soldiers
Conceited dandies
Officially sanctioned terms for the British in
communist East Germany, *c.*1951

**Continental people have a sex life; the English have
hot-water bottles.**
George Mikes, *How to Be an Alien* (1946)

**I'm English and as such I crave disappointment.
That's why I buy Kinder Surprise.**
Bill Bailey

Epping

Imagine our horror walking down Epping High Street in 2005. Nail bar, tanning studio, nail bar, lifestyle consultant, tanning studio, nail bar – and I swear there was even a 'nail bar, tanning studio and lifestyle consultant' rolled into one.

'ExHarlowMan', chavtowns.co.uk, December 2005

Erith

The birthplace of the comedian Linda Smith (1958–2006), who said of it:

It's not twinned with anywhere, but it does have a suicide pact with Dagenham.

Essex

The Anus of England

The map of South-Eastern England looks like the back end of a pig. East Anglia and Kent are the two sides of the rump and Essex occupies a very important position indeed.
Professor Christie Davis, 'The Right to Joke' (2004), Research Report 37 of the Social Affairs Unit

Essex is, of course, home to Essex Man, a self-made, Thatcher-worshipping 'Loadsamoney' type who likes nothing better than to rub his wad in the faces of those less fortunate than himself:
He is a ruthlessly self-interested, philistine, lager-swilling racist and the potential owner of a Rottweiler, if only he had time to walk it.
John Ayto and Ian Crofton, *Brewer's Britain and Ireland* (2005)

The same authors offer the following definition of Essex Girl (who is usually called either Sharon or Tracey):

A type of unintelligent and materialistic young woman who emerged in the late 1980s as the female (but decidedly apolitical) counterpart to Essex Man. Her supposed promiscuity and tarty appearance (short skirt, clunking gold jewellery, white stiletto heels) made her the butt of a variety of politically incorrect jokes (sample: 'How does an Essex Girl turn the light on after sex?' 'She kicks the car door open').

Obviously that is not nearly enough Essex Girl jokes, so here are some more:

Q. How do you make an Essex girl's eyes sparkle?
A. Shine a torch into her ear.

Q. What's the similarity between an Essex girl and a dog turd?
A. The older they get, the easier they are to pick up.

Q. What is the difference between a shopping trolley and an Essex girl?
A. A shopping trolley has a mind of its own.

Q. Why does an Essex girl wear knickers?
A. To keep her ankles warm.

Everton

The city has two great teams. Liverpool and
Liverpool reserves.
Bill Shankly

Princess Margaret: Mr Labone, where is Everton?
Brian Labone (Everton captain): In Liverpool,
   ma'am.
Princess Margaret: We had your first team here
   last year.
Alleged exchange before the 1966 FA Cup Final

Exmoor

'A filthy, barren ground'

So characterized by Daniel Defoe in *A Tour Through the Whole Island of Great Britain* (1724–6), quoting William Camden's *Britannia* (1607)

Eyemouth

Fish guts and stinkin' herr'n' [herring]
Are bread and milk for an Eyemouth bairn [child].
Traditional rhyme, referring to the local fishing industry

Falkirk

F**k**k

So referred to in print by supporters of rival football teams.

Between Glasgow and Edinburgh there's an
unbridgeable gulf – usually called Falkirk.
Saying favoured by both Glaswegians and
Edinburghers

The Fens

Melancholia and self-murder are not unknown in
the Fens. Heavy drinking, madness and sudden acts
of violence are not uncommon.
Graham Swift, *Waterland* (1983). He might have
added incest and witchcraft.

Fife

Cold, Scabby and Grey

Fifers make the rest of Scotland look like a living
sculpture designed to carry across the concepts of
optimism, balance, health and good humour. Cold

scabby bars, cold sea, cold grey hearts, rampant unemployment, cold grey knife-scars, and that's just from the tourist brochure ...
Euan Ferguson, *Observer*, 13 January 2002

There was an old spinster of Fife
Who had never been kissed in her life.
Along came a cat
And she said, 'I'll kiss that,'
But the cat meowed, 'Not on your life!'
Anon.

Fort William

At Fort William they say a Man is not admitted into Society without [a kilt] – the Ladies there have a horror at the indecency of Breeches.
John Keats, letter to Tom Keats (17–21 July 1818)

Frinton-on-Sea

Residents campaigned hard against the opening of a pub in the staid resort, and ice cream cannot be sold on the beach or promenade. This gentility reflects the advanced age of most of the inhabitants – hence the saying:

Harwich for the Continent.
Frinton for the incontinent.

Fulham

Not always the smart place it now is. In the 19th century a Fulham virgin was a prostitute, while in the 1930s Fulham was:

A dismal district … full of pubs, convents, second-hand clothes shops, bagwash laundries and pawnbrokers. Everything seemed very broken down.

John Osborne, *A Better Class of Person* (1981)

Galloway

The people of Galloway … are not all stupid.
Daniel Defoe, *Tour Through the Whole Island of Great Britain* (1724–6)

Galway

'All the barbarities of Ireland'

As in the body natural the crisis of the disease is often made by throwing the peccant humour into the extreme parts, so here the barbarities of Ireland under which it so long laboured, and with which it was so miserably infected, are all accumulated.
John Dunton, letter, 1698

O, the crossbones of Galway,
The hollow grey houses,
The rubbish and the sewage,
The grass grown pier,
And the dredger grumbling

All the night in the harbour ...
Louis MacNeice

Gillingham

Twinned by the local council with the Underworld.
'TheDumbingOfBritain', chavtowns.co.uk, December
2005

Girvan

Cold and inconsequential

**Girvan – a cauld, cauld place. Naebuddy o' ony
consequence was ever born there.**
Robin Ross, *The Chiel* (January 1885)

Glasgow

'This isnae heaven'

After he dies a Glasgow man meets a friend and says, 'Ah'm no sure heaven's such an improvement on Glesca.' His friend says to him, 'This isnae heaven, Jimmy.'

When the Glaswegian economist Adam Smith was boasting about the charms of Glasgow to Dr Johnson, the latter responded:
Pray, Sir, have you ever seen Brentford?
Quoted in James Boswell, *The Life of Samuel Johnson* (1791)

Glasgow, where decay flourishes in a genuinely impressive luxuriance.
Edwin Muir, *Scottish Journey* (1935)

My distant cousin, Mr Leslie Mitchell, once described Glasgow in one of his novels as 'the vomit of a cataleptic commercialism'. But it is more than that. It may be a corpse, but the maggot-swarm upon it is

very fiercely alive. One cannot watch and hear the long beat of traffic down Sauchiehall Street, or see its eddy and spume where St Vincent Street and Renfield Street cross, without realizing what excellent grounds the old-fashioned anthropologist appeared to have for believing that man was by nature a brutish savage, a herd-beast delighting in vocal discordance and orgiastic aural abandon.
Lewis Grassic Gibbon, 'Glasgow'

Rarely have I been so pleased to leave a place.
Luis Cernuda, *Chronicle of a Book* (1958)

The great thing about Glasgow now is that if there's a nuclear attack, it'll look exactly the same afterwards.
Billy Connolly, *Gullible's Travels* (1982), 'Scotland'

If you're staying in a hotel in Glasgow and you phone reception and complain, 'I gotta leak in my sink,' they reply, 'Fine, jist go ahead.'

No soap in Glasgow, oh there is no soap in Glasgow
No soap in Glasgow, oh there is no soap in Glasgow
Chant sung by supporters of Heart of Midlothian,
one of Edinburgh's football teams

**All the wise men come from the East, and all the
cowboys come from the West.**
Edinburgh saying

Grins and Kisses

Glasgow has long had a reputation for aggression
and violence, giving rise to a couple of terms:
- *Glasgow grin:* **a razor slash across the face**
- *Glasgow kiss:* **a head butt**

The infamous Glasgow gangs first hit the head-
lines in the interwar years:
**The gangsters have come to Britain. Glasgow,
second city of the Empire, frankly acknowl-**

edges their reign of terror. A thousand young men … rule the poorer districts. Their insignia of office are the broken bottle, the razor blade, the cosh, the knife and – newest and most effective of all – the bayonet.
Sunday Express, 1935

Q. How many Glaswegians does it take to change a light bulb?
A. None of your fucking business.

A Glaswegian was spotted by his minister leaving a pub. 'Tut, tut,' says the minister, 'and I thought you were a teetotaller.' 'Aye, I am, minister, but no' a bigoted wan.'

When someone was explaining to comedian Ken Dodd the theory of Sigmund Freud that jokes result in elation and relief from tension, he responded: **The trouble with Freud is that he never played the**

Glasgow Empire Saturday night.

There's also the Glasgow Empire joke about the guy who starts juggling with three then four then five balls and gets no applause, so while still juggling he starts to ride a unicycle – still no response – then he's riding the unicycle on a highwire and singing opera arias and now he's juggling six balls – all simultaneously – and there's still complete silence in the auditorium until a grim voice from the back says, 'Is there no end to this man's fuckin' talent?'

The Old Firm

Glasgow is the most sectarian city in the UK outside Northern Ireland, and this is reflected in the city's two main football clubs, Catholic-supported Celtic and Protestant-supported Rangers – known collectively known as the Old Firm. As the journalist Sandy Strang once observed:
A Glaswegian atheist is a bloke who goes to a

Rangers–Celtic match to watch the football.
Then there's this salutary tale:
One night Jimmy's walking across the suspension bridge over the Clyde when he sees a man about to jump into the river.

'Dinnae jump, son,' says Jimmy. 'Think o' yer family.'

'Ah dinnae hae a family,' says the man.

'Then think o' the Rangers.'

'Ah'm no a Rangers supporter.'

'Ach, well think o' Celtic.'

'Ah'm no a Celtic supporter.'

'Ach, in that case,' says Jimmy, 'jump, ye fuckin' atheist.'

Govan

One of Glasgow's toughest areas (one of its estates is known as Wine Alley). Hence the expression:
The best idea since God left Govan.
Andrew Greig, *The Return of John McNab* (1996)

Billy Connolly – taking a cue from the ancient Greeks (who propitiated the Furies by calling them the 'Kindly Ones') – refers to Govan as **'that little fishing village on the Clyde'.**

Gravesend
'A little confused town'

So described by J. Macky in his *Journey thro' England* (1714)

The sewage outfall at Gravesend has given rise to the expression Gravesend twins, meaning … turds.

Great Yarmouth

'Rather spongy and soppy'

It looked rather spongy and soppy, I thought, as I carried my eye over the great dull waste that lay across the river; and I could not help wondering, if the world was really as round as my geography book said, how any part of it came to be so flat. But I reflected that Yarmouth might be situated at one of the poles, which would account for it ...
Charles Dickens, *David Copperfield* (1849–50)

In the Royal Navy to go Yarmouth means to go stark-staring bonkers – from the naval hospital at Great Yarmouth.

Greenock

Looked down on by Glaswegians, who call it Wine City and make such jokes as:

Q. How d'ye tell when a Greenock burd is having
   an orgasm?
A. She draps her fish supper.

Grimsby

You're shit and you smell of fish.
A chant directed at fans of Grimsby Town FC

Undaunted, in 2001 local MP Austin Mitchell
temporarily changed his name to Austin Haddock, to
demonstrate his support for the town's fishing
industry.

Guildford

**Ah, Guildford – the Tunbridge Wells of Surrey, where
Jaguars roam wild and everything stops for gin.**
A.A. Gill, *Sunday Times*, 9 March 2003

Hackney

'Hackney Wick' is rhyming slang for 'prick'.

Haddington

Haddington's most famous daughter had only this to say about the town:

Alas my native place! That Goddess of dullness has strewed on it all her poppies.

Jane Welsh Carlyle, letter to Eliza Stoddart (1824)

Halifax

'It's like Hell, isn't it?'

The painter Edward Wadsworth made this comment to fellow artist Wyndham Lewis while viewing Halifax from the surrounding hills, *c.*1912.

In earlier centuries the magistrates of Halifax enforced the law harshly (often involving the culprit being guillotined on a device called the Maiden of Halifax), giving rise to the famous 'Beggar's Litany':

From Hull, Hell, and Halifax,
Good lord, deliver us.

Daniel Defoe commented, 'How Hull came to be included in this petition, I do not find; for they had no such law there, as I read of.'

Hamilton

'Notoriously a dull place'

Hamilton is notoriously a dull place; if a joke finds its way into our neighbourhood, it is looked upon with as much surprise as a comet would be.
The Hamilton Hedgehog, October 1856

What's Motherwell famous for? Coal and steel.
What's Hamilton famous for? Stealin' coal.
Traditional saying

Hampshire

The inhabitants became known as Hampshire hogs, and were not thought much of by their neighbours: **She was a Dorset woman, and both she and her husband had a profound contempt for what they called the Hampshire hogs with whom they were condemned to live.**
Compton Mackenzie, *My Life and Times* (1963)

Hampstead

When somebody from Hampstead is drowning, all their previous furniture passes in front of them.
Alexei Sayle, quoted in the *Listener*, 1 September 1983

Hampstead did not always have such a moneyed air – in the 19th century the term Hampstead donkeys denoted body lice.

Harlesden

In Harlesden there's a waiting list to get mugged. The only time you would go next door was if you were breaking in.
Shane Richie (Alfie Moon in *EastEnders*), who grew up there, quoted in 2003

Harlow

Much of Harlow's town centre is in a sad state. Empty shops, closing-down sales and a warren of bleak little corners of neglect and decay blight what was once upon a time a visionary social experiment.

   On the street, I stopped people and asked them to sum it up in one word.

   Disappointing; unloved; okay; dirty; shabby; ruined; excellent; shame; crap.
David Sillito, 'Redeveloping Essex's Fallen Utopia', www.news.bbc.co.uk, 16 January 2007

Harrogate

'The queerest place'

The queerest place, with the strangest people in it, leading the oddest lives of dancing, newspaper-reading, and tables d'hôte.
Charles Dickens in 1858

Harrow

Home to one of the country's poshest schools …
At Harrow you could have any boy for a box of Cadbury's milk chocolate.
John Mortimer, quoted in the *Daily Telegraph*, 24 September 1998

Hartlepool

The inhabitants are known as Monkey Hangers, from the time during the Napoleonic Wars when a French ship foundered offshore, and only a monkey survived. Taking this creature for a Frenchman, the benighted Hartlepudlians hanged him.

Even the sea was grim here – not rough, but motionless and oily, a sort of offshore soup made of sewage and poison.
Paul Theroux, *The Kingdom by the Sea* (1983)

Me brother's in borstal,
Me sister's got pox,
Me mother's a whore down Hartlepool docks,
Me uncle's a pervert,
Me aunty's gone mad,
And Jack the Ripper's me dad,
La la la.
Self-disparaging song adopted by Hartlepool fans
in the 1980s

Hastings

'Dreary penance'

We have been dull at Worthing one summer, duller at Brighton another, dullest at Eastbourne, a third, and are at this moment doing dreary penance at – Hastings!

Charles Lamb, *Last Essays of Elia* (1820–3)

Since the 19th century the fortunes of Hastings have somewhat declined, and it is now, with its tatty bedsits full of the impoverished and unemployed, one of the social blackspots of south-east England … It has the second highest divorce rate in the UK.

John Ayto and Ian Crofton, *Brewer's Britain and Ireland* (2005)

A latter-day Dickens would have sketched human tragedy not through the Bridewell but through a Hastings bed and breakfast.

Richard Girling, *Sunday Times*, 23 April 2006

Haworth

'A load of Wuthering Shite'

… you can't stray within 50 miles of Haworth sodding Parsonage without being assailed on all sides by Brontë bilge. The Branwell Tea Shoppe. The Helen Burns Sunbed Centre. Mr Rochester Opticians. Grace Poole Loft Conversions. What a load of Wuthering Shite.

Lucy Mangan, *Guardian*, 5 May 2006

Hayes

'God-forsaken'

One of the most god-forsaken places I have ever struck. The population seems to be entirely made up of clerks who frequent tin-roofed chapels on Sundays and for the rest bolt themselves within doors.

George Orwell, letter to Eleanor Jaques, 1932

Heathrow
'Thiefrow'

So dubbed from the 1970s, from its reputation as a place where large amounts of stuff goes walkabout.

… a beached sky-city, half space station and half shanty town.
J.G. Ballard, *Millennium People* (2003)

Herefordshire
'Hairyfordshire'

A 19th-century slang term for the female pudenda.

Herne Bay
'Hernia Bay'

So called owing to its large community of retirees.

The resort has a bleak bungaloid suburb inappropri-
ately named Stud Hill.

**Herne Bay. Hum. I suppose it is no worse than any
other place in this weather, but it is watery rather,
isn't it? In my mind's eye, I have the sea in a
perpetual state of smallpox; and the chalk running
downhill like town milk.**
Douglas Jerrold, letter to Charles Dickens, June 1843

**And as for Herne Bay, detestable place, I hope we
shall go somewhere else.**
William de Morgan, *Joseph Vance* (1906)

Highgate
A touch reserved …

**Highgate, where couples can sit in cafés waiting for
an introduction before they remember they've been
married for 40 years.**
Euan Ferguson, *Observer*, 10 July 2005

Highlands and Islands
'A frightful country'

It is all one undistinguished range of mountains
and woods, overspread with vast and almost unin-
habited rocks and steeps filled with deer
innumerable ... a frightful country.

Daniel Defoe, *A Tour Through the Whole Island of
Great Britain* (1724–6)

I write you this on my tour through a country where
savage streams tumble over savage mountains, thinly
overspread with savage flocks, which starvingly
support the savage inhabitants.

Robert Burns, letter to Robert Ainslie from Loch
Long, 28 June 1787

Heelandman, Heelandman, where were ye born?
  Up in the Heelands amang the long Corn.
And what grows there, Pray! Why, sibees and leeks,
  *And lang-legged Heelandmen wanting their
    breeks!*

Nursery rhyme ('sibees' = 'spring onions')

Teuchter Jokes

Teuchters – as Glaswegians and other Lowlanders refer to the inhabitants of the Highlands and Islands – are the butt of similar jokes to those told about the Irish.

A Lewis man phones the airline to find out how long it takes to fly from Stornoway to Glasgow.

'Just a minute, sir …' says the man at the airline.

'Thank you very much,' says the Lewis man, and hangs up.

Three steel erectors are working on a new high-rise building in Glasgow. One is from Paisley, one is from Wishaw and the third is from the island of Islay. When they stop for lunch the Paisley man looks at his sandwiches and says, 'Oh no, not cheese and cucumber again. Ah swear Ah'll throw myself aff that girder if Ah get cheese and cucumber in ma piece the morra.' Then the Wishaw man bites into his lunch and groans, 'Ah'm sick o' jam and peanut butter. Ah tell ye, Ah'll be following ye's aff that girder if Ah get jam an peanut butter in ma piece the morra.' Then the Islay man looks at his lunch. 'Och, it'll be another potato santwich, I'm thinking. I too not like potato santwiches at all. If I get another potato santwich tomorrow, I'm thinking I'll pee jumping with you poys.'

The following day at lunch the Paisley man opens up his lunchbox, and without a word walks along the girder and jumps. The Wishaw man bites into his piece, wipes away a tear, and, with the brief 'Ah tell't her,' launches himself into oblivion. Then the Islay man chomps through his sandwich, shouts, 'Potato!' and plummets to his doom.

At the joint funeral the wives are bereft. 'If only Ah'd kent,' sobs the Paisley wife. 'If only he'd tell't me,' wails the woman from Wishaw.

'I ton't unterstand it at all,' says the Islay lass. 'He always mate his own santwiches.'

In Victorian times an English vicar was on a walking tour in the Highlands. It began to rain heavily as he walked down a long and remote glen, and the vicar was glad when he came at last to a small settlement. Knocking on the first door, he opened it a crack and asked, 'Are there any Christians in this house?'

 'No, sir,' came a reply from the smoky darkness. 'We are all Camerons here.'

Holyhead

There is a regular ferry service to Dún Laoghaire in Ireland, and some voyagers have judged that the town has not cheered up much since the early 18th century, when Jonathan Swift described it

as 'scurvy, ill-provided and comfortless'.
John Ayto and Ian Crofton, *Brewer's Britain and Ireland* (2005)

Huddersfield

The inhabitants are the epitome of the taciturn Yorkshire tyke. There is a story of the Huddersfield woman who visits Chartres Cathedral. Looking around the magnificent interior, she appears to be awed into silence. But after a moment or two she declares, 'It'll be a bugger to dust.'

Hull

In 2003 Hull was famously voted Britain's crappest town by readers of the *Idler*. Two years later it came out as worst town in the UK in a Channel 4 programme. An earlier resident agreed:

It's a frightful dump.
Philip Larkin, letter to Robert Conquest, 24 July 1955

In 2006 *Men's Health* magazine produced a report –
based on exam results, numbers of locals with
degrees, and performance in the BBC's *Test the Nation*
IQ test – which concluded that Hull is the most
stupid place in Britain.

Iona
Shite and sanitary towels

Topheavy carrion gulls gape
as they scoop up shite in their beaks
and peck at seapink sanitary towels
in the orange light.
Tom Buchan, 'Iona', from *Dolphins at Cochin* (1969)

American customer: Do you have a map of Ten en a?
Bookseller: Ten en a, sir? Where is that?
American customer: Well, it's a little island off the

west coast of Scotland …
Quoted in 'Bent's Notes', *Bookseller*, 17 January 2003

Ipswich
'27,000 miles from London'

27,000 miles from London nestled deep in the
Suffolk countryside the historic town of Ipswich has
long been regarded as Britain's best kept secret. It
was only after the 1986 Freedom of Information Act
made certain official documents available to the
public that the government admitted that it actually
existed at all.
www.destinationipswich.co.uk

I can't read and I can't write,
But that don't really matter,
Cos I support Ipswich Town,
And I can drive a tractor!
Chant sung by Colchester United fans (and by others
about other places)

Ireland

'Behaving like a lavatory attendant'

Ireland is a modern nation but it was modernized only recently and at the moment it is behaving rather like a lavatory attendant who has just won the lottery.

Terry Eagleton, *The Truth About the Irish* (2001)

What ish my Nation? Ish a villain, a bastard, a knave and a rascal.

Macmorris in William Shakespeare's *Henry V* (III.ii)

I reckon no man is thoroughly miserable unless he be condemn'd to live in Ireland.

Jonathan Swift, letter to Ambrose Philips, 1709

A beautiful country, sir, to live out of!

Thomas Moore

The bane of England, and the opprobrium of Europe.

Benjamin Disraeli, speech, 9 August 1843

'You disapprove of the Swedes?'
'Yes, sir.'
'Why?'
'Their heads are too square, sir.'
'And you disapprove of the Irish?'
'Yes, sir.'
'Why?'
'Because they are Irish, sir.'
P.G. Wodehouse, *The Small Bachelor* (1927)

Among the countless blessings I thank God for,
my failure to find a house in Ireland comes first …
The peasants are malevolent. All their smiles are
false as hell. Their priests are very suitable for
them but not for foreigners. No coal at all. Awful
incompetence everywhere. No native capable of
doing the simplest job.
Evelyn Waugh, letter to Nancy Mitford, 1 May 1952

Charming, soft-voiced, quarrelsome, priest-ridden,
feckless and happily devoid of the slightest integrity
in our stodgy English sense of the word.
Noël Coward, diary, 1960

The Irish don't know what they want and are prepared to fight to the death to get it.
Sydney Littlewood, speech, 13 April 1961

My grandmother took a bath every year, whether she was dirty or not.
Brendan Behan, *Brendan Behan's Island* (1962)

The Irishman, now, our contempt is beneath –
He sleeps in his boots and he lies in his teeth,
He blows up policemen, or so I have heard,
And blames it on Cromwell and William the Third.
Michael Flanders (with Donald Swann), 'A Song of Patriotic Prejudice' from *At the Drop of Another Hat* (1964)

A nation of masturbators under priestly instruction.
Brian Moore (1921–99), Irish novelist

Men have been dying for Ireland since the beginning of time and look at the state of the country.
Frank McCourt, *Angela's Ashes* (1996)

Ireland, the *Big Issue* seller of Europe.
A.A. Gill

*Irish Jokes
Just a few for now ...*

Sure God help the Irish, if it was raining soup, they'd be out with forks.
Brendan Behan, *Brendan Behan's Island* (1962)

Have you heard about the Irishman who had a leg transplant? His welly rejected it.
Frank Carson

Knocking down a house in Dublin recently, the workmen found a skeleton with a medal on a ribbon around its neck. The inscription was: Irish Hide and Seek Champion 1910.
Frank Carson

Two old drunks on their way home from the pub were reeling along a country road in near darkness. 'Seamus, I think we've stumbled into the graveyard – look, I can see a stone here that says a man lived to 105.'

'Glory be Malarky,' the other one exclaims. 'Was it anybody we knew?'

'No, 'twas somebody named "Miles from Dublin".'

Seamus and Sean start work at a sawmill. After an hour Seamus lets out a big yell. 'Help, Sean, I lost me finger!'

Sean says, 'Now how did you go about doing that?'

'Sure I just touched the big spinning job here, just like thi— Feck! There goes another one.'

Seamus says to Sean, 'At me funeral be sure to pour a bottle o' whiskey over me grave.'

'Sure,' says Sean, 'but ye wouldn't mind if it was to pass through me kidneys first?'

Jedburgh

For those crossing into Scotland via the A68 and
Carter Bar, Jedburgh is the first Scottish town they
will come to, and the centre, with its old houses
gaily repainted, offers a welcoming prospect.
Unfortunately this impression is somewhat under-
mined by the notice greeting travellers on the door
of the first café they will encounter in the
Canongate:

> PLEASE NOTE We DO NOT offer, sell or give-
> away TAP WATER Thank you.

This policy is rigorously enforced, even if one is
attempting to deal with the place's thirst-inducing
speciality, 'crispy coated haggis'.

John Ayto and Ian Crofton, *Brewer's Britain and
Ireland* (2005)

Jodrell Bank

The Cheshire village (made famous by the nearby
radio telescope) has, in the contracted form 'Jodrell',
became rhyming slang for 'wank'. Hence a Jodrell
Banker denotes a clapped-out old tart.

Keighley
Good for target practice

**I know the Army needs some place for gunnery
practice, but surely they could find some new and less
visually sensitive location to blow up – Keighley, say.**
Bill Bryson, *Notes from a Small Island* (1995)

Kerry
'The men all savages'

Although the people of County Kerry supposedly say

there are only two kingdoms, the Kingdom of Kerry and the Kingdom of God, visitors in the past found it far from godly:

All acclivity and declivity, without the intervention of a single horizontal; the mountains all rocks, and the men all savages.

Thomas Moore, journal, 6 August 1823

Kerryman Jokes

Kerryman jokes are to the rest of Ireland what Irish jokes are to the English. Here are a few examples:

Q. How would you get a Kerryman onto the roof of a pub?
A. Tell him the drinks are on the house.

Did you hear about the Kerryman who had a brain transplant? The brain rejected him.

Q. How do you keep a Kerryman occupied for
   the day?
A. Give him a piece of paper with nothing but
PTO written on both sides.

A Kerryman, flush with EU subsidies, goes to the
doctor with a crack in his head. 'I'd better sew that
up for you,' says the doctor. 'But first I'll give you a
local anaesthetic.' 'Oh, feck the expense,' says the
Kerryman. 'Give me the imported one!'

Q. What do you call a Kerryman under a wheel-
   barrow?
A. A mechanic.

Did you hear about the Kerryman who found
drinking milk injurious to his health? The cow
collapsed on top of him.

Q. What do you do if a Kerryman throws a pin
   at you?

A. Run like the hounds of hell – he'll have the grenade between his teeth.

Did you hear about the Kerryman who cheated Irish Rail? He bought a return ticket to Dublin and never went back home.

Kettering

Sounds like a Nazi general – Feldmarschal von Kettering, at your service, mein Führer!
Spike Greene

Killarney

A hideous row of houses informed us that we were at Killarney.

W.M. Thackeray (as Michael Angelo Titmarsh), *Irish Sketch-Book* (1843)

Very commercial, very spoilt and of little interest.
Brendan Lehane, *The Companion Guide to Ireland* (2001)

Kilburn

Count your blessings. You could be in Harlesden.
Tom Dyckhoff, *Guardian*, 4 February 2006

Kilmarnock

Kilmarnock, a grimy, tumble-down place with an air of general slatternliness, but full of character …
Edwin Muir, *Scottish Journey* (1935)

The Lake District

'A carpark with puddles'

Lucy Mangan, *Guardian*, 5 May 2006

Here [vice] is flagrant beyond anything I could have looked for: and here while every justice of the peace is filled with disgust and every clergyman with (almost) despair at the drunkenness, quarrelling and extreme licentiousness with women – here is dear good old Wordsworth for ever talking of rural innocence and deprecating any intercourse with towns, lest the purity of his neighbours should be corrupted.
Harriet Martineau, letter from the Lake District to Elizabeth Barrett (1846)

Lampeter

Lampeter ... A city that stays awake all night staring at the ceiling.
Linda Smith, *A Brief History of Time-Wasting*, BBC

Radio 4 (2002)

Lanarkshire

In the dirty business of politics, the linen doesn't wash much dirtier than in Labour's Scottish heartland of Lanarkshire. In recent years the grim Scottish shire has become synonymous with corruption, sectarianism, nepotism, bitter grudges and in-fighting.

Gerard Seenan, *Observer*, 20 October 2002

Lancaster

'Little to recommend it'

The town is ancient; it lies, as it were, in its own ruins, and has little to recommend it but a decayed castle, and a more decayed port ...

Daniel Defoe, *A Tour Through the Whole Island of Great Britain* (1724–6)

Largs

'Smug'

A smug, substantial, modern pleasure resort –
or rather pleasure as the Scots conceive it.
Evelyn Waugh, diary, 13 November 1940

Leeds

Airs above its station

Time was – oh happy time – when Leeds was
content with being Leeds, proud city of Victorian
arcades and Alan Bennett. Now it seems to think it's
Manhattan, or Shanghai, or DanDaresville. It's all
you metrosexuals' fault, with your disposable
income and penchant for truffle oil.
Tom Dyckhoff, *Guardian*, 21 January 2006

The bloke next to me is reading *American Psycho*. It
may well be the only book Leeds fans have ever read.
John Aizlewood, *Playing at Home* (1999)

138

Q. What's the difference between a Leeds fan and
   a coconut?
A. One's thick and hairy, and the other's a tropical
   fruit.

Of Leeds players:
All the qualities of a dog except loyalty.
David Mellor, *Evening Standard*, 23 January 2004

**To many vocal supporters of Leeds United,
'Springtime for Hitler' would be read not as satire,
but as a simple celebration of Nazism. 'Spurs are on
their way to Auschwitz', goes a chant Leeds sing at
White Hart Lane.**
Matthew Norman, *Evening Standard*, 24 January 2005

Leicester

'Boring, boring Leicester!'

Chant sung by Leicester City fans themselves. This is
perhaps a little unfair, as the city can boast not only

the first roundabout in the UK, but the first branch of Tesco outside London (not to mention the first automatic multi-storey car park in Europe).

In his *Guide to England*, Mr Muirhead, in his comfortable fashion, calls [Leicester] 'a busy and cheerful industrial place, for the most part built of red brick,' and for some hours after I had arrived there I found it impossible to improve upon that description and difficult even to amplify it … The town seemed to have no atmosphere of its own. I felt I was quite ready to praise it, but was glad to think I did not live in it.
J.B. Priestley, *English Journey* (1934)

The very reason Joe Orton left Leicester, aside from some rather restricted cottaging opportunities, was its stubbornly starchy culture. Necrophilia wouldn't have gone down well on the city's am-dram scene in the 1960s.
Guardian, 30 November 2002

The university appears to have a chip on its shoulder, if the following joke is anything to go by:

Q. How many Leicester students does it take to change a light bulb?

A. Four. One to change the bulb and three to complain that this sort of thing never happens at Oxford or Cambridge, so could we *please* have some more funding.

Leitrim

'One step beyond the back of beyond'

Traditional description of the Irish county

Lerwick

'Shit creek'

A loose translation of the name Lerwick, which derives from Old Norse *leirr*, 'mud', and *vik*, 'bay'.

It would be difficult to find any place where the citizens are more class conscious – though not in a Marxian sense – more purse-proud, more snooty towards their supposed inferiors.
Hugh MacDiarmid, *Lucky Poet* (1943)

Letchworth Garden City
'Not even energetic enough to be ugly'

I was once again struck by the aesthetic blandness of Letchworth. It's not even energetic enough to be ugly.
A.A. Gill, *The Angry Island* (2006)

Lewisham

I want to go to heaven, but if Jeffrey Archer's there, I want to go to Lewisham.
Spike Milligan

Lichfield

Dr Johnson was a native, and later recalled:
All the decent people got drunk every night and were not the worse thought of.

Lichfield … a nice, dull little place in glazed salmony Midland brick.
V.S. Pritchett in *Why do I Write?* (1948)

Limerick
'Stab City'

This much-resented moniker was awarded to the city in the 1970s following an incident in which a member of one drugs gang stabbed another in the stomach with a pitchfork. Gang violence continued into the 21st century, although the natives (very) defensively point out that there is less serious crime in Limerick than in Cork or Dublin.

Limerick already had a reputation as Ireland's grimmest city when Frank McCourt published *Angela's Ashes* in 1996. Locals were incensed at this memoir of a poverty-ridden childhood in Limerick, accusing McCourt of making things up about his neighbours and exaggerating the deprivation suffered by his own family.

But Limerick already had a bad press, being, according to one traveller in the early 19th century …
The very vilest town.
H.D. Inglis, *A Journey Taken Throughout Ireland during the Spring, Summer and Autumn of 1834* (1835)

A century later it was the same story:
A gloomy little town … everything submerged in vile darkness.
Heinrich Böll in 1950

And another half-century on the press wasn't getting any better:
This sodden city in Western Ireland has been such a hard-luck town that it cannot even lay claim to the

form of verse everyone assumes was named after it.
… Long considered Ireland's most entrenched
Catholic city, it has suffered from stereotyping as
'violent, intolerant, obscurantist and reactionary'.
Warren Hoge, *New York Times*

In some kind of riposte, the editor of the *Limerick
Times* lashed out:
I am sick unto death of obscure English towns that
exist seemingly for the sole accommodation of these
so-called limerick writers – and even sicker of their
residents, all of whom suffer from physical deformi-
ties and spend their time dismembering relatives at
fancy dress balls.

But fellow Irishmen can be just as rude as the English:
For many years we have been campaigning for the
closure of Cork's borders. Reasons for shutting out
Limerick to the north are obvious …
www.peoplesrepublicofcork.com, 19 January 2006

Lincoln

Decayed and dirty

An old dying, decay'd, dirty city.
Daniel Defoe, *A Tour Through the Whole Island of Great Britain* (1724–6)

Liverpool

'Thieves and scallies, rob-dogs and whiners'

Liverpool is undoubtedly the most abused place in the British Isles:

… the venomous derision for Liverpudlians that condemns them as soon as they open their mouths as thieves and scallies, rob-dogs and whiners.
Linda Grant (a Liverpudlian writer), complaining in the *Guardian*, 5 June 2003

A city that often gives the impression of wearing its decline as a badge of honour.
Michael Henderson, *The Times*, 21 November 1998

A Liverpool audience is usually dull.
Charles Dickens, letter, 1862, while on a reading tour

I took a train to Liverpool. They were having a festival of litter when I arrived. Citizens had taken time off from their busy activities to add crisp packets, empty cigarette boxes, and carrier bags to the otherwise bland and neglected landscape. They fluttered gaily in the bushes and brought colour and texture to pavements and gutters. And to think that elsewhere we stick these objects in rubbish bags.
Bill Bryson, *Notes from a Small Island* (1995)

Q. How many work at Liverpool Docks?
A. About half of them.
Told by the Liverpool-born Jimmy Tarbuck at the Palladium in the 1970s

An American journalist visits the Liverpool Docks and sees a docker writhing around in pain. 'What the hell's wrong with him?' he asks. 'He wants to go to the toilet,' says another docker. 'So why doesn't he go?' 'What? On his lunch break?'

Liver Birds

How I love the Marsh Lane girls,
Mascara'd eyes and peroxide curls
I love to kiss those greasy lips,
Just to get the flavour of the curry and chips.
Liverpool Ladies, Liverpool Ladies, Liverpool Ladies,
You're loved the whole world over.
Joe Orford, 'Liverpool Ladies'

Q. What's the definition of confusion?
A. Father's Day in Liverpool.

Scouse toddler to mother, who is doing the
washing-up: Mummy, why are your hands so soft?
Mother: I'm twelve.

People from Liverpool … insist on telling you all the
time how funny they are rather than actually being,
for instance, funny …
Euan Ferguson, *Observer*, 26 January 2003

The inhabitants of the Pool are known as Scousers (from lobscouse, a revolting sailor's stew once popular hereabouts). Alan Bennett (among others) has complained about the Scouse accent:

There is a rising inflection in it, particularly at the end of a sentence, that gives even the most formal exchange a built-in air of grievance.

The more exuberant and youthful natives of Liverpool are also known as Scallies, a usage dating to the 1980s and connoting a certain degree of hooliganism. It is sometimes used admiringly by Liverpudlians of each other (but its use by outsiders tends to be resented).

Perhaps more than any other British city, Liverpool has been the victim of metropolitan disdain:

Do you know, if you wear a flat heel in Liverpool, they think you're a lesbian?
Isabella Blow, fashion director of *Tatler*, quoted in the *Guardian*, 27 November 2002

*The folk that live in Liverpool, their heart is in their
    boots;*
*They go to hell like lambs, they do, because the
    hooter hoots.*
G.K. Chesterton, 'Me Heart'

**You know what Scousers are like, they are always up
to something …**
Jack Straw, then New Labour home secretary, in
April 1999

Boris's Boo-Boo

An anonymous leading article in the *Spectator* of
16 October 2004 opined:

**Liverpool is a handsome city with a tribal sense
of community. A combination of economic
misfortune … and an excessive predilection for
welfarism have created a peculiar, and deeply**

unattractive, psyche among many Liverpudlians. They see themselves whenever possible as victims, and resent their victim status; yet at the same time they wallow in it. Part of this flawed psychological state is that they cannot accept that they might have made any contribution to their misfortunes, but seek rather to blame someone else for it, thereby deepening their sense of shared tribal grievance against the rest of society.

The article went on to berate the people of Liverpool for their public grief over the murder of Ken Bigley, a Liverpudlian engineer held hostage in Iraq, and for denying the role of Liverpool fans in the Hillsborough disaster in 1989, in which 96 Liverpool supporters lost their lives (the *Spectator* diminished this to 'more than 50'). When shortly after the disaster the *Sun* newspaper had made this suggestion (one not upheld by subsequent inquiries) its sales in Liverpool plummeted.

In the wake of the *Spectator* article the magazine's editor, Boris Johnson, Conservative MP for Henley, was ordered by his party leader, Michael Howard, to go to Liverpool to apologize in person. He duly did so, on 20 October 2004, and on a BBC Radio Merseyside phone-in was told by one woman to 'try and be a decent person', while Ken Bigley's brother Paul more robustly called Johnson a 'self-centred pompous twit' and told him to 'get out of public life'.

Shortly after the Boris Johnson affair, Michael Bywater wrote in the *Independent* (21 November 2004):

We all know that Liverpool is a hellish, cold tip of a place populated by self-pitying scallies whose idea of a good time is weeing down a rolled-up copy of the *Echo* at a football match.

Boris Johnson was not the first to identify Liverpool as

SELF-PITY CITY

Jonathan Margolis used this phrase in the *Sunday Times*, 28 February 1993, following scenes of Liverpool mobs throwing stones at the vans carrying the boys accused of Jamie Bulger's murder. Margolis also spoke of Liverpool as 'a paranoia theme park', and of the city's 'incipiently barbaric culture'.

[In the wake of the Hillsborough disaster] the shrine in the Anfield goalmouth, the cursing of the police, all the theatricals, come sweetly to a city which is already the world capital of self-pity. There are soapy politicians to make a pet of Liverpool, and Liverpool itself is always standing by to make a pet of itself. 'Why us? Why are we treated like animals?' To which the plain answer is that a good and sufficient minority of you behave like animals.
Edward Pearce, *The Times*, 23 April 1989

The royal family has taken its whacks with a certain decent cheerfulness, something which compares

interestingly with the intimidatory self-pity issuing from Liverpool if anyone suggests that idle, violent city is, well, an idle, violent city and not a citadel of delightful Scouser wit and defiance.
Guardian, 24 May 1993

It could be argued that it was his [John Lennnon's] narcissistic emoting, never shot through with the tiniest ray of intellectual rigour, which began the Liverpudlianization of Britain and turned us into a country that fills its gutters with tears for girls we've never met.
Euan Ferguson, *Observer*, 20 October 2002, referring to the 1997 Diana grief-fest

Sometimes it can still be the most mind-bogglingly awful and whingeing place, where the glass is always half-empty.
Sir David Henshaw, chief executive of Liverpool City Council, at a conference marketing Liverpool as the 2008 European Capital of Culture

As well as emotionalism, the people are damned

both for their poverty and for their supposedly light fingers:

In your Liverpool slums, in your Liverpool slums
You look in the dustbin for something to eat,
You find a dead rat and you think it's a treat,
In your Liverpool slums.

In your Liverpool slums, in your Liverpool slums
You speak in an accent exceedingly rare,
Wear a pink tracksuit and have curly hair
In your Liverpool slums.

In your Liverpool slums, in your Liverpool slums
Your mum's on the game
And your dad's in the nick
You can't get a job cos you're too fucking thick
In your Liverpool slums.

Sung to the tune 'My Liverpool Home' by supporters of many of Liverpool FC's rival clubs, with considerable variations

Another football chant, sung to the tune of 'You Are My Sunshine':

DON'T GO THERE!

You are a Scouser,
An ugly Scouser,
You're only happy
On Giro day,
Your mum's out thieving,
Your dad's drug-dealing,
So please don't take
My hubcaps away.

Q. What's the difference between Batman and
   a Scouser?
A. Batman can go anywhere without Robin.

Q. Why does the River Mersey run past Liverpool?
A. Because if it went any slower it'd get mugged.

Q. What do you call a Scouser in a suit?
A. The accused.

Even Liverpool's 2003 nomination as European
Capital of Culture in 2008 failed to shift the stereo-
typical Liverpool jokes:
Did you hear about the Pool becoming European

Capital of Culture? Now when they nick your wheels you find your car standing on a set of library books.

Q. What should you do if you see a Scouser jogging?
A. Tackle him and give the lady back her handbag.

Britain has finally decided to assist in the Louisiana disaster zone [following Hurricane Katrina]. We're sending across a group from Liverpool to help with the looting.
Euan Ferguson, *Observer*, 11 September 2005

More Liverpool Jokes

After his first game with Liverpool, the club's new signing, Rigobert Song from Cameroon, rushes to phone his mother to tell her all about it. 'O Rigobert,' she says, 'I am so very, very proud of you, that you are playing for the Once Mighty Reds. But,' and here a quaver enters her voice,

'but here at home things are really really very very
bad. There is so much violence, your sister has
been sexually assaulted twice, your granny has
been robbed in the street and there is raw sewage
running down the gutters. It is getting more and
more like a war zone every day.' She sobs, and
resumes, 'Oh why oh why, Rigobert, did you talk
us into coming to live with you in Liverpool?'

Q: Why will Liverpool never win the League?
A: They keep scoring Owen goals.

A man is walking down a street in the centre
of Manchester when he sees a pit-bull terrier
attacking an old lady. Fearlessly he wades in
and, after receiving many nasty bites, manages
to get his hands round the dog's neck and
presses his fingers in until the dog chokes and
dies. A journalist happens to be passing and
witnesses this heroism, and says to the man,
'That was fantastic, I'm going to write that up

for the paper. I can just see the headline – "Man U Fan in Heroic Rescue". 'Sorry, mate, but I'm not a Man U fan.' 'Oh, OK, how about "City Fan Saves Granny's Life"?' 'No, I'm not a City fan either. I'm from Liverpool.' The journalist's face falls and he walks away. The next morning the man picks up the local Manchester paper and reads the headline: "SCOUSE BASTARD KILLS FAMILY PET".

Liverpool has one great building after another. Why is every one of them next to a shithouse?
US comedian Jackie Gleeson, playing the Liverpool Philharmonic Hall, 6 July 2004

As a final blow to Liverpool's *amour propre*, in October 2004 Julia Baird, the half-sister of John Lennon, Liverpool's most famous son, told the *Chester Chronicle*:
John was very fond of Chester. We always thought it was the place to be, not Liverpool.
Ouch.

Llandudno

'Screams behind closed doors'

Llandudno was the sort of place that inspired old-fashioned fears of seaside crime. It made me think of poisoning and suffocation, screams behind closed doors, creatures scratching at the wainscotting. I imagined constantly that I was hearing the gasps of adulterers from the dark windows …
Paul Theroux, *The Kingdom by the Sea* (1983)

It took me several days to learn how to pronounce Llandudno without choking on my own alveoli.
Vitali Vitaliev, 'Wales', www.travelintelligence.com

Llangollen

Enough to give you toothache

Although the place is now renowned for its international music festival, the quality of the local musicians was not always so high:

Here I am in Wales … a harpist sits in the lobby of every inn of repute playing so-called folk melodies at you – i.e. dreadful, vulgar, fake stuff, and *simultaneously* a hurdy-gurdy is tootling out melodies … it's even given me a toothache.

Felix Mendelssohn, letter to Zelter from Llangollen, 8 August 1829

Llantrisant
'The Hole with the Mint'

So dubbed since the Royal Mint moved here from Tower Hill in 1967.

Lochgelly
Fear and Loathing

The Revd Ron Ferguson gave a collection of his *Herald* columns the title *Fear and Loathing in*

Lochgelly (2003). Perhaps not coincidentally, a 'lochgelly' became a name for the tawse – a leather strap with thongs once used to chastise the children of Scotland (the straps were manufactured here).

The town itself was revealed in a 2004 survey to be the last place in Britain people want to live, in that its house prices are the lowest in the country.
Lochgelly became a byword for gloom. Shops are boarded up; houses lie derelict. Only undertakers and deep-fried food dealers appear to thrive. It is the Scottish mining town they forgot to shut up.
Stephen Khan, *Observer*, 25 January 2004

Loch Lomond

Though to many Scots it is the Queen of Lochs, some visitors from the south have been somewhat sniffy:
Who ever travelled along the banks of Loch-Lomond, variegated as the lower part is by islands, without feeling that a speedier termination of the

long vista of blank water would be acceptable; and
without wishing for an interposition of green
meadows, trees, and cottages, and a sparkling
stream to run by his side?
William Wordsworth, *Topographical Description of the
Country of the Lakes in the North of England* (1810,
revised 1820)

Coleridge (who travelled with the Wordsworths up
Loch Lomond-side in 1803) more succinctly agreed,
remarking:
Every where there is a distressing sense of local
unrememberableness.
Samuel Taylor Coleridge, journal, 25 August 1803

London
'What rubbish!'

Field Marshal Blücher's exclamation on viewing
London from the Monument, June 1814. His remark
(in German '*Was für Plunder!*') is often misquoted as

DON'T GO THERE!

'Was *für plündern!*' ('What a place to plunder!')

I would sell London, if I could find a suitable purchaser.
Richard I in *c.*1189, attempting to raise money for the
Third Crusade, quoted in William of Newburgh,
Historia Rerum Anglicarum (1196–8)

Crowds without company, and dissipation without pleasure.
Edward Gibbon, *Memoirs of My Life* (1796)

**It is a damned place – to be sure – but the only one
in the world (at least in the English world) for fun …**
Lord Byron, letter, 1 March 1816

**The truth is, that in London it is always a sickly
season. Nobody is healthy in London, nobody can be.**
Mr Woodhouse in Jane Austen's *Emma* (1816)

London Cuisine

The bread I eat in London is a deleterious paste, mixed up with chalk, alum and bone-ashes; insipid to the taste, and destructive to the constitution ...

The milk ... the produce of faded cabbage-leaves and sour draff ... frothed with bruised snails, carried through the streets in open pails, exposed to foul rinsings discharged from doors and windows, spittle, snot, and tobacco-quids ... [and so on for the remainder of a lengthy paragraph]

I shall conclude this catalogue of London dainties, with that table-beer, guiltless of hops and malt, vapid and nauseous; much fitter to facilitate the operation of a vomit, than to quench thirst and promote digestion; the tallowy rancid mass called butter, manufactured with candle-grease and kitchen stuff; and their fresh eggs, imported from France and Scotland.

Tobias Smollett, *The Expedition of Humphry Clinker* (1771)

Hell is a city much like London –
A populous and a smoky city;
There are all sorts of people undone,
And there is little or no fun done;
Small justice shown, and still less pity.
Percy Bysshe Shelley, *Peter Bell the Third* (1819)

You are now
In London, that great sea, whose ebb and flow
At once is deaf and loud, and on the shore
Vomits its wrecks, and still howls on for more.
Percy Bysshe Shelley, 'Letter to Maria Gisborne'

But what is to be the fate of the great wen of all? The monster, called ... 'the metropolis of the empire'?
William Cobbett, *Rural Rides* (1822)

A duller spectacle this earth of ours has not to show than a rainy Sunday in London.
Thomas De Quincey, *Confessions of an English Opium Eater* (1822)

London is the grandest and most complicated monstrosity on the face of the earth.
Felix Mendelssohn, letter, 25 April 1829

That monstrous tuberosity of civilized life, the capital of England.
Teufelsdröckh in Thomas Carlyle's *Sartor Resartus* (1833–4)

London is a modern Babylon.
Benjamin Disraeli, *Tancred* (1847)

That great foul city of London there ... rattling, growling, smoking, stinking ... a ghastly heap of fermenting brickwork, pouring out poison at every pore.
John Ruskin, *The Crown of Wild Olives* (1866)

London, black as crows and as noisy as ducks, prudish with all the vices in evidence, everlastingly drunk, in spite of ridiculous laws about drunkenness, immense, though it is really basically only a collection of scandal-mongering boroughs vying with each other, ugly and dull, without any monuments except interminable docks.
Paul Verlaine

London is a large village on the Thames where the principal industries carried on are music halls and the confidence trick.
Dan Leno, music-hall entertainer

London, that great cesspool into which all the loungers of the Empire are irresistibly drained.
Arthur Conan Doyle, *A Study in Scarlet* (1887)

London is too full of fogs – and serious people. Whether the fogs produce the serious people or whether the serious people produce the fogs, I don't know, but the whole thing rather gets on my nerves.
Oscar Wilde, *Lady Windermere's Fan* (1892)

What is London but a vast graveyard of stilled hopes in which the thin gnat-swarm of the present population dances its short day above the daily growing, indisturbable detritus of all the past at rest?
Ford Madox Ford, *The Soul of London* (1905)

London! Pompous Ignorance sits enthroned there and welcomes Pretentious Mediocrity with flattery and gifts. Oh, dull and witless city! Very hell for the restless, inquiring, sensitive soul. Paradise for the snob, the parasite and the prig; the pimp, the placeman and the cheapjack.
James Bridie, *The Anatomist* (1931)

It [New York] seemed almost intolerably shining, secure and well dressed, as though it was continually going out to gay parties while London had to stay at home and do the housework.
Noël Coward in 1943

London fails to look splendid because it is a hard place, as hard as nails.
V.S. Pritchett, *London Perceived* (1962)

When it's three o'clock in New York, it's still 1938
in London.
Bette Midler, quoted in *The Times*, 21 September 1978.
Something similar has been attributed to Groucho Marx.

[A] noisy and extensive scene of crowds without
company, and dissipation without pleasure.
Edward Gibbon, *Memoirs of My Life* (1796)

Goodness me, but isn't London big? It seems to start
about twenty minutes after you leave Dover and just
goes on and on, mile after mile of endless grey
suburbs with their wandering ranks of terraced
houses and stuccoed semis that always look more or
less identical from a train, as if they've been
squeezed out of a very large version of one of those
machines they use to make sausages.
Bill Bryson, *Notes from a Small Island* (1995)

Perhaps the Briony who was walking in the direc-
tion of Balham was the imagined or ghostly
persona. This unreal feeling was heightened when,
after half an hour, she reached another High Street,

more or less the same as the one she had left behind. That was all London was beyond its centre, an agglomeration of dull little towns. She made a resolution never to live in any of them.
Ian McEwan, *Atonement* (2001)

Lurgan

Once again Portadown has beaten Lurgan in the 'quality of life' index, published yesterday by the Northern Ireland Social Trends Survey. Lurgan was officially ranked 'Worst town in Northern Ireland', while Portadown retained its coveted title of 'Worst town in Northern Ireland (excluding Lurgan)'.

Following a series of extensive interviews, questionnaires and RUC undercover operations, Lurgan people are revealed to be consistently uglier, nastier, less intelligent and more inbred than their Portadown counterparts, according to the authoritative report.
Portadown News, a satirical online news sheet (March 2001)

Luton

You *will* want to leave Luton as soon as you arrive …
Stewardess announcement on an easyJet flight from
Berlin to Luton, 1 February 2005, prior to outlining
her company's car-hire operation.

**A town seemingly twinned with the seventh circle
of hell.**
Tom Dyckhoff, *Guardian*, 12 February 2005

Luton was voted Britain's crappest place to live in
Crap Towns II (2004).

Maidenhead

'Too snobby to be pleasant'

**Maidenhead itself is too snobby to be pleasant.
It is the haunt of the river swell and his overdressed
female companion. It is the town of showy hotels,
patronized chiefly by dudes and ballet girls. It is the**

witch's kitchen from which go forth those demons of the river – steam-launches. *The London Journal* duke always has his 'little place' at Maidenhead; and the heroine of the three-volume novel always dines there when she goes out on the spree with somebody else's husband.

Jerome K. Jerome, *Three Men in a Boat* (1889)

In 2003 a confidential social profile used by the Department of Work and Pensions described it (much to the fury of the locals) as:

Somewhat spoiled by the gin and Jag brigade.

Maidstone

Er … there's a crater on Mars named after it …

Manchester

'This Foul Drain'

In the days when Manchester was Cottonopolis, the world capital of the textile industry, a French visitor had this to say:

From this foul drain the greatest stream of human industry flows out to fertilize the whole world. From this filthy sewer pure gold flows. Here humanity attains its most complete development and its most brutish; here civilization makes its miracles, and civilized man is turned back almost into a savage.

Alexis de Tocqueville, *Journeys to England and Ireland* (1835)

A German resident, who ran his family's cotton mill in the city, had a similarly high opinion of the place:

Masses of refuse, offal and sickening filth lie among standing pools in all directions; the atmosphere is poisoned by the effluvia from these, and laden and darkened by the smoke of a dozen tall factory chimneys. A horde of ragged women and children swarm about here, as filthy as the swine that thrive upon

**the garbage heaps and in the puddles … The race
that lives in these ruinous cottages, behind broken
windows, mended with oilskin, sprung doors, and
rotten door-posts, or in dark, wet cellars, in meas-
ureless filth and stench, in this atmosphere penned
in as if with a purpose, this race must really have
reached the lowest stage of humanity.**
Friedrich Engels, *The Condition of the Working Class
in England* (1845)

A solution to the Manchester Problem was offered
in 1930:
**The shortest way out of Manchester is notoriously
a bottle of Gordon's gin.**
William Bolitho, *Twelve Against the Gods*, 'Caliogstro
and Seraphina' (1930)

Commentators these days tend to look for more
desperate remedies:
**Don't bomb Iraq
Nuke Manchester**
Banner displayed by fans of Liverpool FC in 2003

Manchester has fancied itself rotten for as long as anyone can remember.
Stuart Maconie, *Pies and Prejudice* (2007)

MADchester

During Manchester's flirtation with the hip, hot and happening club scene in the later 1980s and 1990s – when it produced such bands as The Smiths, The Stone Roses, Happy Mondays and Oasis – it became known as Madchester, a pun on MDMA, the scientific abbreviation for the drug Ecstasy.

I would like to live in Manchester. The transition between Manchester and Death would be unnoticeable.
Mark Twain

Mancunians ... make an affectation of candour and trade a little on their county's reputation for

uncouthness.
Harold Brighouse, *Hobson's Choice* (1917)

He chose to live in Manchester, a totally incomprehensible choice for any free human being to make.
Sir Melford Stevenson, judge, quoted in the *Daily Telegraph*, 11 April 1979

Manchester … has a compulsion to preen and show off. It is narcissistic, contrary and wayward …
Chris Lethbridge, 'Change and Contradiction', *Diverse City* (1994)

There's only one Harold Shipman,
There's only one Harold Shipman,
There's only one Harold Shipman …
We've gotta give thanks
Cos he only kills Mancs …
Chant sung by Liverpool fans, referring to the Manchester GP who murdered hundreds of his patients

Come to Sunny Manchester

I arrived in a shower, in the wet now set off,
Eight days in the place I remained:
Seven days, seven nights and a quarter, I vow,
By Jove! it incessantly rained.
…

May Manchester flourish! and if once again
By chance I should ere be brought hither,
I hope that from weeping the clouds may
*   refrain,*
And grant me a peep at fine weather.
Anon., *Manchester Chronicle*, 1821

I looked out of the train window and all I could see was rain and fog. 'I know I'm going to love Manchester,' I told Jim, 'if I can only see it.'
Mae West, *Goodness Had Nothing To Do With It* (1959)

Some Man U Jokes

Q: How many Man United fans does it take to change a light bulb?

A: 560,001. That is 1 to change it, 60,000 to say they've been changing it for years and 500,000 to buy the replica kit.

Q. Can you name three football clubs with a rude word in their name?

A. Arsenal, Scunthorpe, and fucking Manchester United.

Q: What's the difference between Alex Ferguson and God?

A: God doesn't think he's Alex Ferguson.

Manchester United have got a new sponsor: Calvin Klein. Their strips will now read **MUCK**.

... and a Couple of Manchester City Jokes

Q. What do the letters of EIDOS, Manchester City's sponsor, stand for?

A. Eleven Idiots Dreaming of Success.

There are three types of Oxo cubes. Light brown for chicken stock, dark brown for beef stock, and light blue for laughing stock.

This one originated in 1988 with Tommy Docherty. The reference is to City's strip.

Margate

'A most dismal hole'

... finally reached Margate, a most dismal hole, where the iodine and ozone were flavoured with lodgings. I made at once for the railway station and

demanded the next train. 'Where to?' said the official. 'Anywhere,' I replied, 'provided it be far inland.'
George Bernard Shaw, *Star*, 1888

But you think Margate more lively – so is a Cheshire cheese full of mites more lively than a sound one, but that very liveliness only proves its rottenness. I remember too that Margate tho' full of company, was generally filled with such company, as people who were nice in the choice of their company, were rather fearful of keeping company with.
William Cowper, letter, 1763

I left Ramsgate to my right about three miles, and went across the island to Margate; but that place is so thickly settled with stock-jobbing cuckolds, at this time of year, that, having no fancy to get their horns stuck into me, I turned away to my left when I got within about half a mile of the town.
William Cobbett, *Rural Rides* (1820s)

Other men can take their wives half over the world; but you think it quite enough to bring me down here

to this hole of a place, where I know every pebble on
the beach like an old acquaintance – where there's
nothing to be seen but the same machines – the same
jetty – the same donkeys – the same everything.
Douglas Jerrold, 'Mrs Caudle's Curtain Lectures'
(1846)

There is something not exactly high-class in the
name of Margate. Sixpenny teas are suggested, and a
vulgar flavour of shrimps floats unbidden in the air.
Marie Corelli, *Cameos* (1896)

I am very glad you went to Margate, which, I believe,
is the nom-de-plume of Ramsgate. It is a nice quiet
spot not vulgarized by crowds of literary people.
Oscar Wilde, letter, 1898

There's no money in Margate. Eye contact has
replaced it as the root of all evil and, yes, this town's
as ripe as ever for a low-budget remake of *Brighton
Rock:* the joyless amusement arcades, the facial
scars ...
David Seabrook, *All the Devils Are Here* (2002)

Mid-Calder

The village that got an ASBO

In December 2005 the West Lothian village was made
subject to a police dispersal order, following frequent
disturbances by gangs of youths drawn in from the
surrounding area. One local resident who thought the
whole thing was an overreaction complained:
**We are being made out to be the village of the
damned.**

Middlesbrough

'The Los Angeles of the North'

So-called from its absence of culture. The extensive
chemical works hereabouts have led to the inhabitants being labelled Smoggies.

**Middlesbrough, truly the town that time forgot.
Sometimes I half expect Doug McClure to come
running round a corner being hotly pursued by**

Neanderthals, only in this nightmare they are dressed in tracksuits and cheap jewellery.
'johnny_ringo', chavtowns.co.uk, September 2005

Those who say it doesn't deserve the reputation it has ... obviously need to get out just a bit more.
'ontap', chavtowns.co.uk, September 2005

On Middlesbrough FC signing Fabrizio Ravanelli:
Like someone buying a Ferrari without having a garage.
Giancarlo Galavotti, Italian sports writer, 1996

The Midlands
'Sodden and unkind'

When I am living in the Midlands
That are sodden and unkind.
Hilaire Belloc, 'The South Country' (1910)

All his life he's been a citizen of the East Midlands ... By the metropolis's jeering estimates, of course,

these are … a series of worthy, yes, but oh how
meanly parochial dullsvilles.
The Times, 5 December 1980

Holidaymaking Midlanders were a particular bugbear
of one grumpy old man resident in Somerset:
**The roads of West Somerset are jammed as never
before with caravans from Birmingham and the
West Midlands. Their horrible occupants only come
down here to search for a place where they can go to
the lavatory free. Then they return to Birmingham,
boasting in their hideous flat voices how much
money they have saved … Few of these repulsive
creatures in caravans are Christians, I imagine, but I
would happily spend the rest of my days composing
epitaphs for them in exchange for a suitable fee:**

HE HAD A SHIT ON GWENNAP HEAD,
IT COST HIM NOTHING. NOW HE'S DEAD.
HE LEFT A TURD ON PORLOCK HILL.
AS HE LIES HERE, IT LIES THERE STILL.
Auberon Waugh, *Private Eye*, 11 June 1976

Milton Keynes

'Satan's lay-by'

So dubbed by the comedian Bill Bailey.

I didn't hate Milton Keynes immediately, which I suppose is as much as you could hope for the place.
Bill Bryson, *Notes from a Small Island* (1995)

It was built to be modern, efficient, healthy, and, all in all, a pleasant place to live. Many Britons find this amusing.
Neil Gaiman and Terry Pratchett, *Good Omens* (1990)

You can stick your Milton Keynes up your arse.
Chant sung to the tune of 'She'll Be Coming Round the Mountain' by Wimbledon fans enraged by the relocation of their club to Milton Keynes

Morecambe

'Bradford-by-the-Sea'

So named because of the thousands of mill workers

who once came here on holiday every year.

One visitor has inscrutably observed that the town has
All the virtues of Buda, and all the vices of Pest.

**The surprising thing about Morecambe … isn't that
it declined, but that it ever prospered. It would be
hard to imagine a less likely place for a resort. Its
beaches consist of horrible gooey mud and its vast
bay spends large periods devoid of water …**
Bill Bryson, *Notes from a Small Island* (1995)

Morningside
'Where sex is what the coal comes in.'

One of the interesting results of the famous
Morningside accent.

**Day by day, one new villa, one new object of offence,
is added to another; all around Newington and
Morningside, the dismalest structures keep
springing up like mushrooms … They belong to**

no style of art, only to a form of business much to
be regretted.
Robert Louis Stevenson, *Picturesque Notes on
Edinburgh* (1879)

Motherwell

As the town slid into despondency following the
closure of the vast Ravenscraig steelworks in the early
1990s, rival football fans began to sing:
If you've got a job to go to, clap your hands …
(to the tune of 'She'll Be Coming Round the
Mountain')

Neasden

*'The eminently mockable epitome of suburban
futility'*

**The satirical magazine *Private Eye* homed in on it in
the 1960s as the eminently mockable epitome of**

possess a certain nasal narrowness that fits it well
for the role too. Central to the Private Eye Neasden
saga is the spectacularly unsuccessful local football
club, created by the magazine's Peter Cook and
Barry Fantoni, with its cast of grotesques: the
manager, tight-lipped ashen-faced Ron Knee; the
heavy-scoring centre forward Pevsner (all own-
goals, unfortunately); the fan club (Sid and Doris
Bonkers).

John Ayto and Ian Crofton, *Brewer's Britain and
Ireland* (2005)

Neasden,
You won't be sorry that you breezed in,
The traffic lights and yellow lines,
And the illuminated signs,
All say welcome to the borough that everyone's
    pleased in.

Willie Rushton, 'Neasden'

Neath

'The bag-snatching capital of Wales'

Dylan Thomas's description of the place, following a rugby match involving Neath RFC:

In the game there were at least five instances of people being grabbed by the testicles. Neath is the bag-snatching capital of Wales.

Newcastle upon Tyne

'A Toon Called Malice'

Headline in the *Mirror*, January 2005, following the spat at Newcastle United between Craig Bellamy and Graeme Souness

Queen Victoria, as she approached the city by train, pointedly drew the blinds. The equally refined fans of Middlesbrough FC chant:

You're just a shite town on Tyneside.

… while Freddie Shepherd, a director of Newcastle United, has opined (much to the wrath of Geordies and Geordettes):
Newcastle girls are all dogs.

Geordettes

What are they? 'Worra you mean, what are we? Wanna slap? I'll tell you who we are. Only the most bang up for it lasses in the entire land, like. Wanna piece of it? Do you? Do you?' And with that, the flesh-devouring, bottle-crunching womenfolk of Newcastle go braying into the town centre. Men scatter as the micro-skirted Valkyries descend on Weatherspoon's. A surprising 80% of Geordie blokes reckon that, on an average night out in Newcastle, they've had their drinks spiked by man-eating babes and then been date-raped. Who knows how many victims will be claimed tonight? Bar

bouncers tremble, there's panic in the barracks,
footballers refuse to go out without the latest in
anti-date-rape technology in their handbags,
bejewelled chavs on their way to urinate over
Debenhams turn through 180 degrees and run
home to their mummies. The police have urged
victims to come forward. Their stories will be
treated in confidence and counselling will be
available.

Hermione Eyre and William Donaldson,
A Dictionary of National Celebrity (2005)

Me Muthor-in-Law. Mind she's a hard un. We tuk
her alang te one o' these open-air zoos one day,
Flamingo Park. Suddenly ah luks aroond an' there
she wasn't. 'Wheors yor muthor gone?' ah sez te wor
lass. 'Where, Dickie?' she sez, 'ye knaa – she's away
ahint one them trees – ye knaa – te pooder hor nose.'
'Ye fond bee,' ah sez, 'thors lions runnin' aboot in
theor.' Just then ah hears a dreadful roarin' soond.
'What ye ganna dee?' sez wor lass. Ah points tiv a

tree and theor wez a lion up on the highest branch
and me muthor-in-law stannin' at the foot o' the
tree. 'The lion got itsell into that mess,' ah sez, 'it can
get itsell oot.'
Dick Irwin, *100 Geordie Jokes* (1990)

Knock knock.
Who's there?
Geordie.
Geordie who?
Geordie-rectly to jail, do not pass Go, do not collect
£200.

Newhaven

Newhaven is spot and rash and pimple and blister;
with the incessant cars like lice.
Virginia Woolf, diary, 1921. Woolf lived nearby.

Newquay

I don't know if you've been to Newquay before, but in my view, attempting to have a fun weekend in Newquay is a contradiction in terms.
Judge Jeffrey Rucker, sentencing two young visitors who attacked a couple of Newquay residents, 3 January 2006

Norfolk
'Very Flat'

Very flat, Norfolk.
Noël Coward, *Private Lives* (1930)

NFN
'Normal For Norfolk'; abbreviation used by medical practitioners. In urban myth, incest is a popular pastime in the county, hence the alleged high levels of mental deficiency.

This is Norfolk. You get applause for standing up straight.
Sue Townsend, *Adrian Mole: The Cappuccino Years*
(dramatization on BBC TV, 2001)

Norfolk people themselves might say of one of their less-gifted own:
Dunt git no further than Wensday.

People who live in Norfolk (1):
Forever measuring their dining-rooms before driving into Diss with a view to bidding for a refectory table at a Saturday morning furniture auction.
A definition in William Donaldson's *Dictionary of Received Ideas* (2003)

People who live in Norfolk (2):
Norfolk folk of a more rustic bent are inclined when they meet each other abroad to offer the greeting:
He' yer fa' got a dickey, bor?
('Has your father got a donkey, boy?')
To which the other will wittily respond:

Yis, an' he want a fule ter roid 'im, will yew cum?
('Yes, and he wants a fool to ride him, will you come?')

Turkeys and Bedbugs

In the 19th century people from Norfolk were jeeringly known as Norfolk Turkeys, on account of their supposed lack of mental agility … and the county's poultry industry.

Also in the 19th century bedbugs were called Norfolk Howards, apparently in mockery of a man called Joseph Bug, who, embarrassed at his name, changed it to 'Norfolk Howard', probably inspired by the fact that the family name of the dukes of Norfolk is Howard.

The North

'It's grim up North'

Traditional saying

Northerners are far too busy breeding pigeons, eating deep-fried chip butties and executing drive-by shootings on Moss Side to dally over the new Sebastian Faulks.
Hildy Johnson, *Bookseller*, 9 March 2001

People in the North die of ignorance and crisps.
Edwina Currie, speaking as junior health minister, September 1986 (Currie is herself from Liverpool).

Down the pub Friday night
Getting absolutely plastered
Go back home and beat your wife
You dirty northern bastards.
Chant sung by supporters of clubs from southern England

DON'T GO THERE!

Northampton

Cobblers!

Northampton Town FC are nicknamed the Cobblers because of the town's long association with shoe-making. Among the club's former players is … Des O'Connor.

In 2005 the town's Greyfriars Bus Station was named the worst transport station in the UK on Channel 4's *Demolition* programme.

Re the 'David Syndrome', identified by Italian psychologist Graziella Magherini to 'encompass the feelings of sensory overload from viewing too much art in Florence', a native of Northampton, D.B.C. Reed, wrote to the *Guardian* (16 November 2005) to say: **Visitors to Northampton are guaranteed to escape this unpleasant experience.**

Northern Ireland

'Down with the whole damn lot!'

Down with the bold Sinn Fein!
We'll rout them willy-nilly,
They flaunt their crimes
In the Belfast Times,
Which makes us look so silly.
Down with the Ulster men!
They don't know which from what.
If Ireland sunk beneath the sea
How peaceful everyone would be!
You haven't said a word about the RUC?
Down with the whole damn lot!
Noël Coward, 'Down with the Whole Damn Lot',
song from *Co-optimists* (1920s)

For generations, a wide range of shooting in
Northern Ireland has provided all sections of the
population with a pastime which … has occupied a
great deal of leisure time. Unlike many other countries, the outstanding characteristic of the sport has
been that it was not confined to any one class.
Northern Ireland Tourist Board, 1969

For God's sake, someone bring me a large Scotch. What a bloody awful country.
Reginald Maudling, Conservative Home Secretary, reported comment on a flight back to London, 1 July 1970

Anyone who isn't confused here doesn't really understand what's going on.
Anon. Belfast citizen, remark to journalist, 1970

The Irish don't know what they want and won't be happy till they get it.
British army officer, 1975

They should never have shared the Nobel Peace Prize between two people from Northern Ireland. They will only fight over it.
Graham Norton

Norwich

'Merely a manufacturing town'

So dismissed by Andrew Robertson in 1812, in a letter to the painter John Constable

On the inbreeding tendencies of Norfolk folk:

Q. How did the Norwich man find his sister in the wood?
A. Just fine.

This kind of thing inevitably has an effect on the local intelligence quotient:
Two Norwich fans are walking along the street. One of them picks up a mirror, looks in it and says, 'Hey, I know that bloke!' The second one picks it up, looks into the mirror and says, 'Of course you do, you idiot – it's me!'

Q. What's a mile long with an IQ of 45?
A. A parade in Norwich.

Delia Smith offered to send the Norwich players on a luxurious holiday in the Caribbean, but they said they'd rather go to Blackpool, as they'd never been on an open-top bus.

It was somehow sadly inevitable that Alan Partridge should have ended his career working for Radio Norwich …

Nottingham
'That dismal town'

So-called by D.H. Lawrence in his poem 'Nottingham's New University'. Other sobriquets include Shottingham and Assassination City, both coined by the tabloids in response to the high murder rate in the city in the early 21st century.

There once was a baker of Nottingham
Who in making éclairs would put snot in 'em.
  When he ran out of snot

He would, like as not,
Take his pecker and jack off a shot in 'em.

Actually, Nottingham originally was called Snottingham, from the Anglo-Saxon for 'homestead of the people of a man called Snot'. Who Snot was history does not record, for time, like a handkerchief made of Nottingham lace, has blown away all trace of him.

All Nottingham has is Robin Hood, and he's dead.
Bryan Roy, on leaving Nottingham Forest in 1997. He forgot to mention the mass-murdering GP Harold Shipman, who was born here.

Nottingham Forest Jokes

A Forest fan says to his mate, 'What would you do if you won the lottery?' And his mate answers, 'No doubt there, I'd buy a controlling interest in the club.' 'OK,' says his mate, 'but

what if you got four numbers up?'

Q. What do the Premiership and Brazil have
in common?
A. Soon neither of them will have Forest.

Q. Why do NASA send their astronauts to train
at Forest's City ground?
A. It's the only place on earth with no atmosphere.

Nottingham was recently judged the second worst
town in England by some television property
pundits, which makes me wonder whether
Kingston-upon-Hull could really be so bad. Nothing
has disturbed the view I formed four years ago that
it has the ugliest provincial city centre I have ever
seen, designed without care, or feeling, or even
eyesight, such is its encrustation of visual pollution.
Nottingham actually doesn't deserve a cricket
ground as pretty as Trent Bridge, which was today
as lovely as I remembered it: Gaddafi Stadium

would better suit the environs.
Gideon Haigh, cricinfo.com, 25 August 2005

Nottingham was once known for being primarily subterranean, with most of its citizens living in the sandstone caves that still riddle the city. Slightly ironic, because many of its current denizens seem to have regressed to troglodyte tendencies …
Nottingham is rapidly becoming a putrid tumour of social rot in the heart of England.
'jdennis_99', chavtowns.co.uk, January 2006

Notting Hill
'Rotting Hill'

So called by the painter and writer Wyndham Lewis, who lived in Notting Hill Gate in the 1940s, and published a critique of the decay of England under this title in 1951. Of course, it's all gone very much upmarket since then, thanks to Hugh and Julia. It is now the home of metrosexual Tories, also known as Notting Hillbillies.

Oldham

Oldham Athletic? That's a contradiction in terms.
Line from an old episode of *Coronation Street*

Oxford
'A complete dump'

Line spoke by Stephen Fry (a Cambridge graduate) in
Blackadder Goes Forth (1990). For Richard Ingrams,
former editor of *Private Eye* and himself an Oxford
man, the place is:
**Just a lot of men in duffel coats wandering up and
down the High Street.**

**Oxford accent … the strangulated effete drawl of
the upper-middle-class intellectual (or booby).**
John Ayto and Ian Crofton, *Brewer's Britain and
Ireland* (2005)

Oxford University is known by Cambridge students

as Cowley Polytechnic, or, from the dark blue worn
by Oxford University sports teams, as The Dark Side.

**To the university of Oxford I acknowledge no obli-
gation; and she will as cheerfully renounce me for a
son, as I am willing to disclaim her for a mother. I
spent fourteen months at Magdalen College; they
proved the fourteen months the most idle and
unprofitable of my whole life.**
Edward Gibbon, *Memoirs of My Life* (1796)

**You will hear more good things on the outside of a
stagecoach from London to Oxford than if you were
to pass a twelvemonth with the undergraduates, or
heads of colleges, of that famous university.**
William Hazlitt, *Table Talk* (1821)

**Today Papa has gone to Oxford to see how Bertie
[the future Edward VII] is getting on in that old
monkish place which I have a horror of.**
Queen Victoria, remark, 31 October 1859

I have the greatest respect for the university and its

800 years of tireless intellectual toil, but I must confess that I'm not entirely clear what it's for, now that Britain no longer needs colonial administrators who can quip in Latin.

Bill Bryson, *Notes from a Small Island* (1995)

Parp Parp!

The clever men at Oxford
Know all that there is to be knowed.
But they none of them know one half as much
As intelligent Mr Toad!

Kenneth Grahame, *The Wind in the Willows* (1908)

All things bright and beautiful,
All creatures great and small,
Swindon rule the West Country
And Oxford rule fuck all,
Fuck all, fuck all, fuck all.

Chant sung by fans of Swindon Town FC

Paisley
'A dirty, filthy hole'

In 1870 one observer held that Paisley was:
The dirtiest and most unhealthy town in Scotland.
Around the same time another visitor complained of
its 'drunken squalor and puritanical religion'. In 2007,
nearly a century and half later, a Paisley native opined
to the *Scotsman* newspaper that the town was still:
**A dirty, filthy hole of a place to live in. The only good
thing about Paisley is there's plenty of transport to
Glasgow.**

Perhaps not entirely incidentally, the expression
'To get off at Paisley' means to perform coitus inter-
ruptus, Paisley being the last station on the West
Coast line before Glasgow.

Paisley's football club is St Mirren (named after the
saint who founded Paisley's first church in the 6th
century).
**A footballer died and arrived at the gates of heaven
where an angel awaited him. 'Now,' said the angel,**

'before you enter here, is there anything that happened to you on earth upon which you would like your mind set at rest?' The footballer thought for a moment and then said, 'There is one matter. I belonged to the famous St Mirren Club and one cup final when we were playing the Rangers, I scored a goal which I am sure was offside. It won us the match and the cup, but I've always been troubled about it.' 'Oh,' replied the angel, 'we know all about that goal up here; it was perfectly right, so you can banish all your doubts.' 'Oh, thank you, St Peter,' said the footballer. The angel replied, 'But I'm not St Peter, you know.' 'Then who are you?' asked the footballer. 'St Mirren,' came the reply.

Partick

For years I thought the club's name was Partick Thistle Nil.
Billy Connolly, himself a native of Partick
As a small boy I was torn between two ambitions: to

be a footballer or to run away and join a circus. At
Partick Thistle I got to do both.

Alan Hansen, who formerly played for the Jags, in 1997

Peacehaven

What is one to say? Peacehaven has been called a
rash on the countryside. It is that, and there is no
worse in England.

Nikolaus Pevsner, *The Buildings of England: Sussex* (1965)

Peterborough

Yes, Peterborough, where lives are lived in a blaze
of obscurity. Where all emotion is laid bare and
then hastily covered up in case anyone should see,
like too much white flesh on a Spanish beach.

Fiona Fowler, 'Dancing Housewives'

It's horrible, and not in a funny way, just a bad way. I wrote the entire book without going there and then went for a night to check a few details. I stayed at a hotel. There's nothing I can say apart from: don't do that. I tried to go to a restaurant; there are no restaurants in Peterborough.

Mark Haddon, who set his novel *A Spot of Bother* in Peterborough, quoted in the *Observer*, 27 August 2006. Asked if he was worried about a backlash, Haddon shrugged. 'They'd be too lethargic,' he said.

Plymouth

Plymouth is a seaside city unlike any other … even the seagulls seem more forlorn, malicious and evil than those you may have encountered before.

'massey', chavtowns.co.uk, September 2005

The city's football team has given rise to a piece of criminal rhyming slang: Plymouth Argyle = file (the sort smuggled into prison in a cake).

[Plymouth] Argyle is normally virtually invincible at home, partly because by the time the opposing side has travelled all the way to Plymouth, they've usually given up.

h2g2, www.bbc.co.uk, 21 February 2003

Pontypridd

Q. How many people does it take to change a light bulb in Pontypridd?

A. Ten. One to buy the light bulb and nine to petition the government for the electrification of Pontypridd.

Portland

If you like your life bleak as a Mike Leigh film, and don't mind averting your eyes from quarry scars and godawful houses, Portland is paradise.

Tom Dyckhoff, *Guardian*, 7 January 2006

Portsmouth

'Belligerence and stubbornness'

There's a kind of clannishness within Pompey, built on family after family, which has led to this feeling of belligerence and stubbornness. It's quite a secret place, square-shouldered, right-angled and deeply unpretty. It has a kind of gruff charm when you get to know it. It's very functional. And it's uncursed by money.

Graham Hurley, local author of crime thrillers set in Portsmouth, quoted on anvil.clara.net

Portsmouth is the only British city that was originally an island …

I bet people are wondering why they connected it to the mainland and didn't let it just drift away.

'irnbru4878', chavtowns.co.uk, October 2005

Much of Portsmouth's city-centre post-war rebuilding had a gloom-inducing quality. A notable icon is Owen Lauder's 1966 Tricorn shopping centre, a grimly brutalist example of the architectural style known

214

as 'rough concrete' which was regularly voted one of Britain's least loved buildings. Having been refused a preservation order, it was demolished in 2004. The decision is likely to have delighted Prince Charles, who once described the (long-derelict) building as 'a mildewed lump of elephant droppings'.
John Ayto and Ian Crofton, *Brewer's Britain and Ireland* (2005)

The necessity of living in the midst of the diabolical citizens of Portsmouth is a real and unavoidable calamity. It is a doubt to me if there is such another collection of demons on the whole earth.
General James Wolfe in 1758

One of the most depressed towns in southern England, a place that is arguably too full of drugs, obesity, underachievement and Labour MPs.
Boris Johnson, *GQ*, May 2007

Defence Secretary Geoff Hoon should have consulted the book [a guidebook to Britain] before opining in the House of Commons last week that 'Umm Qasr is a city similar to Southampton'. A British squaddie was quick to correct him, explaining: 'Umm Qasr has no beer, no prostitutes and people are shooting at us. It's more like Portsmouth.'

Observer, 30 March 2003. The bit about 'no prostitutes' is something of a puzzle, given that this naval port (nicknamed Pompey) is renowned for them, to the extent that 'Pompey whore' is, among the rougher sort of bingo caller, rhyming slang for twenty-four.

The Skates

Southampton supporters call Pompey supporters 'Skates', as a result of a fanzine competition to find something that would really get up the noses of their rivals. Portsmouth people themselves had long called seamen 'skates', from the old story that sailors who had been too long at sea would release their sexual tension using a skate nailed to the mast.

> Portsmouth FC's ground at Fratton Park gives
> the anagram:
> **Krap, Nott Arf**

Poundbury

Prince Charles's Toy Town in Gloucestershire is not to
everybody's taste:

**This neurotic, irritably sighing, obsessively curated,
wilfully blinkered suburb.**
A.A. Gill, *The Angry Island* (2006)

**A twee fantasy of pre-industrial England that filters
out plague and poverty but grafts on garages, cars
and telly.**
Edwin Heathcote, *Financial Times*, 29 February 2005

**Prince Charles's village just seems to wish it was
back in 1750, like an aged relative who sees you as**

an adult and somehow can't help but wish you were who you were 30 years ago.
Alain de Boton, quoted in the *Observer*, 23 April 2006

Preston

Not much to say except …
We all hate Preston!
We all hate Preston!
We all hate Preston!
Chant favoured by Blackpool supporters, who have wittily renamed Preston North End FC, Preston Knob End

Their supporters often refer to their club as PNE, an acronym made from their initials but which to most people sounds like a sexually transmitted disease.
The Alternative Blackpool Website
(www.localdial.com/users/soulbrother/bpool/preston
12.htm)

The UK's first motorway, opened in 1958, must have had a similar aversion to the place: it was the Preston Bypass. Colonel Saunders was less discerning: the UK's first branch of Kentucky Fried Chicken was opened in Preston's Fishergate.

Misattributed Quotes

The Alternative Blackpool Website has come up with some variations on well-known quotations:

Deepdale [Preston's ground] is the home of lost causes, forsaken beliefs, unpopular names and impossible loyalties.
Attributed to 'Anyone who has ever seen them'

The difference between supporting Preston and death is that with death you can do it alone and no one is going to make fun of you.
Attributed to Woody Allen

Preston is a town united in its delusion about its heritage and a common hatred of its neighbour.
Attributed to Dean William R. Inge

It is only when watching Preston that I truly remember how tragic the world really is.
Attributed to Robert Lynch

Ramsgate

'Ramsgate the asinine'

Margate the shrimpy, Ramsgate the asinine, Canterbury the ecclesiastical.
George Sala, *Twice Round the Clock* (1859)

There were no lodgings at Ramsgate (thank Heaven!) ...
Charles Dickens, letter to John Forster, September 1839

I warn you against Ramsgate, which is a strip of London come out for an airing.
George Eliot, letter, 4 July 1852

We leave Ramsgate, then, with its 'stuckuppishness' and stiff and formal society.
Chambers Journal (1853)

Karl Marx took his family there for a holiday in 1864, and his jaundiced view of the place was perhaps influenced by the eruption of a carbuncle just above his penis:
Your philistine on the spree lords it here as do, to an even greater extent, his better half and his female offspring. It is almost sad to see venerable Oceanus, that age-old Titan, having to suffer these pygmies to disport themselves on his phiz [physiognomy, i.e. face], and serve them for entertainment.
Karl Marx, letter to Friedrich Engels, 25 July 1864

At this moment Ramsgate is populated almost exclusively by small GREENGROCERS and other quite small SHOPKEEPERS from London … At first

sight one would think they were working men, but their conversation immediately betrays the fact that they are RATHER ABOVE THAT and belong to QUITE THE MOST DISAGREEABLE STRATUM OF LONDON SOCIETY – they're the kind who, in speech and manner, are already preparing themselves, after the inevitably pending bankruptcy, for the no less inevitably impending career of COSTER-MONGER.
Friedrich Engels, letter to Karl Marx, 25 August 1876

Reading
'Such a dull town'

In response to Logan Pearsall Smith's well-known aphorism, 'People say that life's the thing, but I prefer reading,' the poet John Betjeman is alleged to have remarked:
What did he see in Reading? It's such a dull town.

The river is dirty and dismal here. One does not linger in the neighbourhood of Reading.
Jerome K. Jerome, *Three Men in a Boat* (1888)

São Paulo is like Reading, only much further way.
Peter Fleming, *Brazilian Adventure* (1933). São Paulo is generally regarded as a big, boring, anonymous sort of city.

Redditch

Blair Babe Jacqui Smith, MP for Redditch, a Midlands town consistently voted the most boring place to live in Britain, is in sunny mood. For the fourth year running, the town has published a powerfully enervating calendar – The Roundabouts of Redditch – which highlights some of its more exciting traffic islands. 'It's even better than ever,' purrs Smith.
Observer, 28 December 2003

Rhyl

Due for demolition

A town only a man driving a crane with a demolition ball would visit with a smile.
A.A. Gill, quoted in the *Observer*, 20 October 2002

Of this whole stretch of coast – around Rhyl and Prestatyn – Bill Bryson has written:
North Wales looked like holiday hell – endless ranks of prison-camp caravan parks standing in fields in the middle of a lonely, windbeaten nowhere, on the wrong side of the railway line and a merciless dual carriageway, with views over a boundless estuary of moist sand dotted with treacherous-looking sinkholes and, far off, a distant smear of sea … full of Liverpool turds.
Notes from a Small Island (1995)

Anything you can do in Rhyl you can do better elsewhere.
The Rough Guide to Wales. Not to be outdone, *The Times* has described Rhyl as:

Britain's first shanty town.

Rochdale

'Somehow, I can't see you in Rochdale,' I say a bit sadly, probably because I can hardly see myself there any more.
　'Oh, why?' she demands.
　'The shops are not elegant, Virginie. No nice scarves. You would be a gazelle in a cement factory.'
Vikram Seth, *An Equal Music* (1999)

Rochester

Charles Dickens fictionalized the town as Dullborough and Mudfog, which does not bode well (although Dickens lived in Rochester in later life). In Dickens's time the phrase 'Rochester portion' was a euphemism for vagina.

Romford

'A byword for all that is naff and dumbed-down in today's Britain'

Romford. Sometimes it seems almost to have become a byword for all that is naff and dumbed-down in today's Britain. In the media the town is portrayed as a place of drunkenness and violence. People who have never been here make it the butt of their jokes and speak of it with scorn. Sadly it seems that even some who live in the town are beginning to believe the stereotype. Now of course Romford is far from perfect …

Some special pleading from the website www.rom4d.org.uk, which carries the banner: 'Romford: Display Your Pride in the Town'

Rotherham

Apparently the antithesis of metropolitan chic:
You're not from New York City, you're from Rotherham

So get off the bandwagon …
Arctic Monkeys, 'Fake Tales of San Francisco', from
Whatever People Say I Am, That's What I'm Not
(2006). The Arctic Monkeys are a Sheffield band.

Bollocks to Rotherham

On 7 April 2000 Agence France-Presse filed the
following story:
**A gang of thieves who were ordered to plant
daffodil bulbs as part of their community service
have seen their revenge flourish this spring.**

**The group were told to plant hundreds of
bulbs along one of the main roads in
Rotherham, in northern England, last autumn
but, when the bulbs sprouted this week, the
blooms spelled out the words 'Bollocks' and
'Shag' in letters four feet (1.3 metres) wide.**

**Residents living on East Bawtry Road, which
carries thousands of visitors a day, said people**

were coming from miles around to take a look at the flowers.

One, Alan McCue, 48, said, 'I can see the funny side but it doesn't really create a good impression of the town. They planted hundreds of bulbs so we're all a bit worried about what might come up next.'

Rothesay

Half a million fleas

Rothesay, the main town on the island of Bute, has been a popular holiday destination for Glaswegians since the 19th century, although not all the facilities on offer are of the five-star variety:

In search of lodgins we did slide,
To find a place where we could bide,
There was eighty-twa o' us inside
In a single room in Rothesay, O.

We a' lay doon tae tak our ease,
When somebody happened for tae sneeze –
An' he wakened hauf a million fleas
In a single room in Rothesay, O.
Anon., 'The Day We Went to Rothesay, O'

Of Bute itself, Lorraine Davidson, the former New
Labour spin doctor, has said:
I can't think of anything more ghastly.
Broadcasting House, BBC Radio 4, 22 January 2006

Rutherglen

Pronounced Ruggy or Ruglen by the locals – possibly
due to the unpronouncability of Rutherglen after
sniffing glue or consuming 4 bottles of Buckfast …
For anyone thinking of visiting Ruggy you should
plan this like you would a visit to Saddam Hussein's
hometown in Iraq. When I drive through it on my
way home I always park up on the outskirts and
wait for a police car to drive by. Quickly pull out and

follow it through hoping you can make it along the main street without a traffic light change. Public transport through Rutherglen isn't an option. I have seen buses stoned, drivers spat on and am fairly certain one night there was even a failed rocket-propelled grenade attack on the Number 12.
'terminedor', chavtowns.co.uk, December 2005

Rutland

Rutland, the small and some might think obsolete county.
Stuart Jeffries, *Guardian*, 14 December 2005

St Albans

'Vomit, violence and vandalism.'

Mr Eric Roberts, vice-chairman of St Albans Civic Society, characterizes the city's night life, November 2002

St Andrews

When it blows there, even the seagulls walk.
Nick Faldo

The university is a favourite destination for upper-class English 'Yahs' such as Prince William, hence the joke:
Q. How many St Andrews students does it take to change a light bulb?
A. Three. One to call the butler and two to arrange a tailor in Rome to design and make new suits for the special occasion.

St Ives

The Vicar of St Ives says the smell of fish there is sometimes so terrific as to stop the church clock.
Francis Kilvert, diary, 21 July 1870

Sale

I am convinced that the loss of Sale would cause the national IQ level to rise.
'JoePineapples', chavtowns.co.uk, September 2005

Salford
'Dirty old town'

So called in the 1949 song by Ewan MacColl:
I met my love by the gasworks wall,
Dreamed a dream by the old canal,
Kissed my girl by the factory wall,
Dirty old town,
Dirty old town.

No one knows misery like Morrissey, which is why he had The Smiths photographed outside the Salford Lads Club … Salford city centre … whose forlorn demeanour suggests instead a stage set for a post-apocalyptic TV drama … heaven knows

I'm miserable now.
Tom Dyckhoff, *Guardian*, 8 October 2005

Saltcoats

The Ayrshire novelist John Galt (1779–1839)
described the people of Saltcoats as 'a sordid race'.

Scotland
'Full of drunks'

… according to a *Lonely Planet* guide a few years
back, courting publicity … Some time before, an
exiled native characterized the place thus:

A land of meanness, sophistry and mist.
Each breeze from foggy mount and marshy plain
Dilutes with drivel every drizzly brain.
Lord Byron, 'The Curse of Minerva'

Had Cain been Scot, God would have changed his
  doom
Not forced him wander, but confined him home.
John Cleveland (1613–58), 'The Rebel Scot'

**In all my travels I never met with any one
Scotchman but what was a man of sense: I believe
everybody of that country that has any, leaves it as
fast as they can.**
Francis Lockier (1668–1740), English churchman and
writer, quoted in Joseph Spence, *Anecdotes* (1820)

**That garret of the earth – that knuckle-end of
England – that land of Calvin, oatcakes and sulphur.**
Sydney Smith, quoted in Lady Holland, *A Memoir of
Sydney Smith* (1855)

No McTavish
Was ever lavish.
Ogden Nash, 'Genealogical Reflection', *Hard Lines* (1931)

Dr Johnson on Scotland and the Scots

In his *Life of Samuel Johnson* (1791) James Boswell, a Scot, gleefully recorded his friend's animadversions regarding his country and his countrymen.

Seeing Scotland, Madam, is only seeing a worse England. It is seeing the flower fade away to the naked stalk.

God made it, but we must remember that He made it for Scotchmen; and comparisons are odious, but God made Hell.

Much ... may be made of a Scotchman, if he be caught young.

Their learning is like bread in a besieged town: every man gets a little, but no man gets a full meal.

Sir, let me tell you, the noblest prospect which a Scotchman ever sees is the high road that leads him to England.

Boswell: I do indeed come from Scotland, but I cannot help it …
Johnson: That, Sir, I find, is what a very great many of your countrymen cannot help.

Sir, it is not so much to be lamented that Old England is lost, as that the Scotch have found it.

A Scotchman must be a very sturdy moralist who does not love Scotland better than truth.
A Journey to the Western Islands of Scotland (1775)

The Scotsman is mean, as we're all well aware,
And bony, and blotchy, and covered with hair,
He eats salted porridge, he works all the day,
And he hasn't got Bishops to show him the way.

Michael Flanders (with Donald Swann), 'A Song of Patriotic Prejudice', from *At the Drop of Another Hat* (1964)

O Knox he was a bad man
he split the Scottish mind.
The one half he made cruel
and the other half unkind.
Alan Jackson

Racial characteristics: **Sour, stingy, depressing beggars who parade around in schoolgirls' skirts with nothing on underneath. Their fumbled attempt at speaking the English language has been a source of amusement for five centuries, and their idiot music has been dreaded by those not blessed with deafness for at least as long.**
P.J. O'Rourke, 'Foreigners Around the World', *National Lampoon*, 1976

Joke? What Joke?

The whole nation hitherto has been void of wit and humour, and even incapable of relishing it.
Horace Walpole, letter to Sir Horace Mann, 1778

It requires a surgical operation to get a joke well into a Scotch understanding.
Sydney Smith, quoted in Lady Holland, *A Memoir of Sydney Smith* (1855). In J.M. Barrie's play *What Every Woman Knows* these lines are quoted, and a puzzled Scotsman replies, 'What beats me, Maggie, is how you could insert a joke with an operation.'

He is the fine gentleman whose father toils with a muck-fork … He is the bandy-legged lout from Tullietudlescleugh, who, after a childhood of intimacy with the cesspool and the crab louse, and twelve months at 'the college' on moneys wrung from the diet of his family, drops his threadbare kilt and

comes south in a slop suit to instruct the English in
the arts of civilization and in the English language.
T.W.H. Crosland, *The Unspeakable Scot* (1902)

The Irish are great talkers
Persuasive and disarming,
You can say lots and lots
Against the Scots –
But at least they're never charming!
Gavin Ewart, *The Complete Little Ones* (1986)

We're ruled by effete arseholes. What does that make
us? The lowest of the fuckin' low, the scum of the
earth. The most wretched, servile, miserable pathetic
trash that was ever shat intae creation. Ah don't hate
the English. They just git oan wi the shite thuv goat.
Ah hate the Scots.
Irvine Welsh, *Trainspotting* (1993)

A sparsely populated appendage of England … [in
terms of sport] the Belarus of the West.
Professor Nial Ferguson (an expatriate Scot), quoted
in the *Guardian*, 13 January 2006

Scottish Lonely Hearts

Aberdeen man, 50, in desperate need of a ride.
Anything considered. Box 06/03

Heavy drinker, 35, Glasgow area, seeks gorgeous
sex addict interested in pints, fags, Celtic football club and starting scraps on Sauchiehall
Street at three in the morning. Box 73/82

Bitter, disillusioned Dundonian lately rejected
by long-time fiancée seeks decent, honest, reli-
able woman, if such a thing still exists in this
cruel world of hatchet-faced bitches. Box 53/41

Ginger-haired Partick troublemaker, gets slit-
eyed and shirty after a few scoops, seeks
attractive, wealthy lady for bail purposes,
maybe more. Box 84/87

Artistic Edinburgh woman, 53, petite, loves
rainy walks on the beach, writing poetry,
unusual sea-shells and interesting brown rice
dishes, seeks mystic dreamer for companion-
ship, back rubs and more as we bounce along
like little tumbling clouds on life's beautiful
crazy journey. Strong stomach essential. Box
12/32

Bad-tempered, foul-mouthed old bastard living
in a damp cottage in the arse end of Orkney
seeks attractive 21-year old blonde lady with big
chest. Box 40/27

Devil-worshipper, Stirling area, seeks like-
minded lady for wining and dining, good
conversation, dancing, romantic walks and
slaughtering dogs in cemeteries at midnight
under the flinty light of a pale moon. Box 52/07

Attractive brunette, Maryhill area, winner of

Miss Wrangler competition at Framptons
Nightclub, Maryhill, in September 1978, seeks
nostalgic man who's not afraid to cry, for long
nights spent comfort-drinking and listening to
old Abba records. Please, Please! Box 30/41

Govan man, 27, medium build, brown hair, blue
eyes, seeks alibi for the night of February 27
between 8 p.m. and 11.30 p.m.

Scunthorpe

'Who put the c**t in Scunthorpe?'

Old joke. In 1996 AOL's smut-filter prevented web
searches for the town. A similar fate was suffered by
Chorlton-cum-Hardy.

Sheffield

Home of the Dee-Dahs

The natives of Sheffield are so called (as in 'la di dah')
by the people of Rotherham, Barnsley and Doncaster
(which must be very rough places indeed if they think
Sheffield is posh).

**Even Wigan is beautiful compared with Sheffield.
Sheffield, I suppose, could justly claim to be called
the ugliest town in the Old World: its inhabitants,
who want it to be pre-eminent in everything, very
likely do make that claim for it. It has a population
of half a million and it contains fewer decent buildings than the average East Anglian village of five
hundred. And the stench!**
George Orwell, *The Road to Wigan Pier* (1937)

**Wife beating may be socially acceptable in Sheffield
but it is a different matter in Cheltenham.**
Lord Justice Lawton (b.1911), attributed

Sheffield … a great place to leave, but an even better place to avoid.
'GothDude78', chavtowns.co.uk, January 2006

Monday, Tuesday, who the fuck are Wednesday?
Chant favoured by fans of Manchester United

Hard as nails Sheffield, where heterosexual men openly call each other 'Love' and the Village People bandit moustache has never gone out of fashion …
Matt Bennett, 'Sophistication? I've been to Leeds', www.news.bbc.co.uk, 2 August 2001

Shrewsbury

'You're Welsh and you know you are.'

Chant favoured by visiting football supporters, aimed at the fans of Shrewsbury Town

Skegness

'The second biggest arsehole in Britain'

The TV chef Gordon Ramsay, quoted in the *Guardian*,
18 June 2005. He didn't say which was the biggest.

Skelmersdale

**A toxic human landfill site ... a post-holocaust
world truly abandoned by God ... rows of eyesore
concrete terraces huddle together like 'the dead
propping up the dead' ... The only way to prevent
oneself from believing that your optic nerve only
records the colour grey is to focus on the multi-
coloured broken glass and dog shit that covers the
pavements like an inland sea ... It rather brings to
mind the idea that someone has dumped a ripped
bin bag full of crap onto a pristine bowling green.**
'elgringo', chavtowns.co.uk, November 2005

Slough

Not fit for humans

Come, friendly bombs, and fall on Slough
It isn't fit for humans now,
There isn't grass to graze a cow
Swarm over, Death!
John Betjeman, 'Slough', *Continual Dew* (1937)

In a letter of 15 January 1967 Betjeman explained the nature of his loathing:

The town of Slough was not, when those verses were written, such a congestion as it is now and I was most certainly not thinking of it but of the Trading Estate, which had originated in a dump that now stretches practically from Reading to London. The chain stores were only then just beginning to deface the High Street, but already the world of 'executives' with little moustaches, smooth cars and smooth manners and ruthless methods was planted in my mind along the fronts of those Trading Estate factories.

To the accused, Lord Justice Melford Stevenson of the

High Court once said:
**I see you come from Slough. It is a terrible place.
You can go back there.**

**Competing with Keats's 'And no birds sing' as the
most depressing phrase in the English language is
that which one hears as the train draws into the
station: 'Slough, this is Slough.'**
Bill Murphy, *Home Truths* (2000)

Happiness is Slough in my rear-view mirror.
Bumper sticker

The town appropriately enough became the setting
for Wernham Hogg, David Brent's stationery firm in
Ricky Gervais's TV comedy series *The Office*
(2001–3).

**I grew up in Buckinghamshire, quite near Slough,
which I know has been glamorized by *The Office*.
It's not actually that good.**
Jimmy Carr, interview in the *Observer*, 5 December
2004. On another occasion Carr said:

I was born in Slough in the 1970s, if you want to know what Slough was like in the 1970s, go there now.

In a 2007 survey by the Campaign to Protect Rural England to find the most tranquil council area in the country, Northumberland came out top, with a score of 28.6, while Slough, with a score of minus 79.5, came bottom.

Soho

A mile of thwarted, exploited, avaricious and cruel little backrooms made nastier by the daytime presence of the film, TV and advertising industries.
A.A. Gill, *The Angry Island* (2006)

Solihull

**I saw Solyhill; but in it, setting aside the church,
there is nothing worth sight.**
William Camden, *Britannia* (1596)

Southampton
'Scumhampton'

So dubbed by supporters of Portsmouth FC, who
refer to their local rivals as 'Scummers':
**Scummer: those supporting Southampton football
club. *See also:* crap; hate; full of shit; tripe eating;
living in a barn.**
'Thesaurus', pompeyonline.com

The term is said to go back to a dock strike, when the
Southampton dockers went back to work before those
from Portsmouth. It is also said that SCUM was the
acronym of the name of the Southampton dockers'
union at the time: 'Southampton Company of Union

Men'. However, all this is probably apocryphal.

Here is one of many anti-Scummer football chants (of the sort readily adapted to any club):
If you all hate the Scummers clap your hands
If you all hate the Scummers clap your hands
If you all hate the Scummers, all hate the Scummers,
All hate the Scummers clap your hands.

Southend-on-Sea

Rhyming slang for pee or wee

Southend isn't really on the sea but the Thames estuary. Like you couldn't tell from the garbage- and muck-strewn 'beach'. Parents can often be seen trying to pretend they have taken their kids to a real seaside resort by putting them in swimming costumes and helping them build pebblecastles. But no one dares enter the stagnant puddle-water that is the sea … If you can brave the whole day, then watch with awe as Southend transforms into the Monaco grand prix by night, as boy racers zoom up and down the seafront in their Ford Fiestas, mowing down hapless tourists.

Diana McCar, *Guardian*, 28 June 2006

Southwold

Nothing but second homes and B&Bs for people who are scouting for second homes. Southwold has a 60-seat arts cinema, for God's sake. For a population of 52. There are probably bylaws against watching DVDs in case you slip in a Jerry Bruckheimer and the whole place has to be walled up to prevent low culture spreading to Orford and Aldeburgh

Lucy Mangan, *Guardian*, 5 May 2006

DON'T GO THERE!

Stockport

One of the duskiest, smokiest holes in the whole of the industrial area.
Friedrich Engels, letter, 1844

Stoke on Trent
'Is Stoke a dump?'

Title of chat forum on 'Where I Live', bbc.co.uk. One contributor talks of
Drab and dreary built-up areas covered in graffiti and litter, rude and obnoxious locals ...
while to another it is
A very sad place with a very sad future.
Some of the contributors even felt that Stoke should change its name (St Modwen on Trent was suggested by one) in the hope that things might pick up after a re-brand. But as Manchester City fans sing (to the tune of 'Go West'):

You're Stoke
You're a fucking joke.

One of the districts of Stoke was named Etruria by
Josiah Wedgwood when he set up his pottery works
here in the 18th century. It seems no better than the
rest of the city …
I am an Etruscan girl, born and bred, and my mum
told me that in the Second World War hardly any
bombs were dropped on Etruria because the
German bombers would take one look, think they
had already bombed it and move on to Coventry.
Mollie Hemens, letter to the *Guardian*, 21 November
2005

Stow on the Wold

Stow … thinks it's a little smug HobNob stuck in a
tin of dog biscuits … It knows it's the honey-dipped
bollocks … the worst place in the world.
A.A. Gill, *The Angry Island* (2006)

Sunderland

Home to the Stadium of Shite

… as Newcastle fans dub Sunderland FC's Stadium of Light

In fact, Geordies have a real antipathy to their neighbours (known as Mackems), as the following jokes attest:

Q. How does a Mackem change a light bulb?
A. He asks the prison guard.

Q. What do you call a Mackem girl's cleavage?
A. Silicon Valley.

Q. How do you know a Mackem has burgled your house?
A. The bin's empty and the cat's pregnant.

Q. What happens when a Mackem takes Viagra?
A. He gets a bit taller.

Q. What's the difference between a Mackem lass and
 a pit bull?
A. Lipstick.

Surrey

The patio of England

If Kent is the garden of England, then Surrey is
the patio.
Jeremy Clarkson, *Sunday Times*, 3 March 2003

Surrey is viewed as a land of limited horizons, small
ambitions, conventional assumptions, conservative
outlooks, self-satisfied uniformity – a bit like
Switzerland without the Alps (although it does have
Box Hill).
John Ayto and Ian Crofton, *Brewer's Britain and
Ireland* (2005)

Surrey is full of rich stockbrokers, company-
promoters, bookies, judges, newspaper proprietors.

Sort of people who fence the paths across their parks
… They do something to the old places – I don't
known what they do – but instantly the countryside
becomes a villadom … Those Surrey people are not
properly English at all. They are strenuous. You have
to get on or get out. And they play golf in a large,
expensive, thorough way because it's the thing to do.
H.G. Wells, *Mr Britling Sees It Through* (1916)

Swansea
The soggiest city

With an average of 1360.8 mm (53 inches) of rain per
year, Swansea is the wettest city in Britain.

Swansea was a vast cankered valley of sorrowful
houses and grey churches and shut-down factories.
I thought: No wonder the Welsh are religious!
Paul Theroux, *The Kingdom by the Sea* (1983)

Cheer up, Swansea's worse than you.

Chant aimed at Cardiff City supporters by Wrexham fans

According to *The Lonely Planet Guide to Wales* (2nd edition, 2004):
Swansea is an ashtray of a place, with grids of grey streets and morose neighbourhood pubs frantically competing for the Most Miserable award.

Swindon
'Swine-don'

So named by its many friends. Somewhat in the same vein, there is the story of the schoolchild who wrote, 'The Vikings comed from Norway, Swindon and Denmark.' In 2002 the *Guardian*'s architecture and design critic Jonathan Glancey outraged Swindoners by characterizing the place as
A kitsch horror
… while in Mark Haddon's best-selling, Whitbread-Prize winning novel *The Curious Incident of the Dog*

in the Night Time (2003) Swindon is, quite simply
The Arse of the World.

Those in agreement with these views might well sing
along with Oxford United fans:
Swindon Town is falling down,
Falling down, falling down,
Swindon Town is falling down,
Fuck off Swindon.
(To the tune of 'London Bridge is Falling Down')

Thurso

**The big event in Thurso … was in 1834 when Sir
John Sinclair, a local worthy, coined the term 'statis-
tics' in the town, though things have calmed down
considerably since.**
Bill Bryson, *Notes from a Small Island* (1995)

Tipperary

We had now entered the notorious county of
Tipperary, in which more murders and assaults are
committed in one year than in the whole Kingdom
of Saxony in five.

Johann Georg Kohl, *Ireland, Scotland and England*
(1844)

'It's in Tipperary – not at all a desirable county
to live in.'
   'Oh, dear, no! Don't they murder the people?'
Anthony Trollope, *The Eustace Diamonds* (1872)

Tooting

In 2005 the Tooting-reared NASA astronomer Pete
Mouginis-Mark named a crater on Mars after his
home town, leading to many jokes about the place
being barren, lifeless and without much atmosphere.
One journalist responded thus:

It is difficult to know which is further from fashion-
able London: the surface of Mars or the southern
extremities of the Northern line ... Who hasn't ever
dreamed of putting Tooting into outer space?
Andrew Brown, *Guardian*, 2 November 2005

Wales
'My fathers can have it'

The land of my fathers – my fathers can have it.
Dylan Thomas, quoted in *Adam* magazine, December
1953

A country of woodland and pasture ... [which]
breeds men of an animal type, naturally swift
footed, accustomed to war, volatile always in
breaking their word as in changing their abode.
Gesta Stephani, 12th century

It is because of their sins, and more particularly the
wicked and detestable vice of homosexuality, that

the Welsh were punished by God and so lost first
Troy and then Britain.
Gerald of Wales (aka Giraldus Cambrensis), *The
Description of Wales* (*c.*1194)

Taffy was a Welshman, Taffy was a thief,
Taffy came into my house and stole a side of beef.
English nursery rhyme

A Welshman is a man who prays on his knees on
Sundays and preys on his neighbours all the rest
of the week.
Anon.

The earth contains no race of human beings so
totally vile and worthless as the Welsh.
Walter Savage Landor, letter to Robert Southey

The Welsh are so damn Welsh that it looks like
affectation.
Walter Raleigh (1861–1922), letter to D.B. Wyndham
Lewis

'We can trace almost all the disasters of English history to the influence of Wales' … 'The Welsh,' said the Doctor, 'are the only nation in the world that has produced no graphic or plastic art, no architecture, no drama. They just sing,' he said with disgust, 'sing and blow down wind instruments of plated silver.'
Dr Fagan in Evelyn Waugh's *Decline and Fall* (1928)

An impotent people,
Sick with inbreeding,
Worrying the carcase of an old song.
R.S. Thomas, 'Welsh Landscape' (1955)

The Welshman's dishonest, he cheats when he can,
And little and dark – more like monkey than man,
He works underground with a lamp in his hat,
And he sings far too loud, far too often, and flat.
Michael Flanders (with Donald Swann), 'A Song of Patriotic Prejudice', from *At the Drop of Another Hat* (1964)

Gloomy, mountainous, and green

Wales, which I have never seen,
Is gloomy, mountainous, and green,
And, as I judge from reading Borrow,
The people there rejoice in sorrow …
The weather veers from dull to foul,
The letter W's a vowel.
Rolfe Humphries, the US poet, 'For My
Ancestors', *Collected Poems* (1965)

The Welsh are not meant to go out in the sun.
They start to photosynthesize.
Rhys Ifans

Each section of the British Isles has its own way
of laughing, except Wales, which doesn't.
Stephen Leacock

There are still parts of Wales where the only

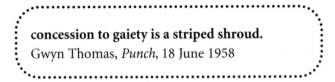

concession to gaiety is a striped shroud.
Gwyn Thomas, *Punch*, 18 June 1958

The Welsh are a nation of male voice choir lovers whose only hobbies are rugby and romantic involvement with sheep.
Lenny Henry

What are they *for*?
Anne Robinson, consigning the Welsh to Room 101 in the eponymous BBC TV programme, March 2001. Robinson also described the Welsh as 'irritating and annoying', adding, 'They are always so pleased with themselves.' The comments aroused fury and accusations of racism from Welsh MPs.

The Welsh have never made any significant contribution to any branch of knowledge, culture or entertainment. They have no architecture, no gastronomic tradition, no literature worthy of the name.

A.N. Wilson, quoted in the *Observer*, 20 October
2002. On another occasion A.A. Gill commented:
**Finding out that your sister is black is fine; finding
out that your sister is Welsh is another thing.**

**You can easily travel from Cardiff to Anglesey
without ever stimulating a taste bud.**
A.A. Gill, quoted in the *Observer*, 20 October 2002

Here Be Dragons

**The ordinary women of Wales are generally
short and squat, ill-favoured and nasty.**
David Mallet (1705–65), letter to Alexander Pope

**Welshmen prize their women so highly that
they put a picture of their mother-in-law on the
national flag.**
Anon. The symbol on the Welsh flag is, of course,
a dragon.

Wallasey

'A 'ole called Wallasey'

We dug the Mersey Tunnel, boys, way back in '33,
Dug a hole in the ground until we found a 'ole called
* Wallasey.*
The foreman cried, 'Get on outside; the roof is
* falling down.'*
And I'm telling you, Jack, we all swam back to dear
* old Liverpool Town.*
Anon., 'I Wish I Was Back in Liverpool'

Walsall

'Walsall – not as bad as you'd think ...'

Motto of www.walsallwonderland.co.uk. The site goes
on to claim the place is 'one of the largest and least
rubbish of England's many rubbish small towns'.

Free entertainment is put on in the town centre on most weekend evenings. The majority is provided by the student population of the town and their inability to oversee the coexistence of five pints of lager and a doner kebab in the same part of their digestive tract.

Open-air late-night boxing is also popular on Friday and Saturday nights, with bouts being arranged at very short notice, usually round about chucking-out time.

www.walsallwonderland.co.uk

A Small town in Poland

Small town in Poland,
You're just a small town in Poland.
Chant sung by opposing football fans, to the tune of 'Guantanamera'

When talking to someone from the town, DO NOT on any account respond to a mention of

Walsall by saying, 'What, the capital of Poland?'
Recent research showed that every resident of
the town has heard this lame joke more than
250 times by the time they are 40 years old.
Most of us have also received a postcard from
Warsaw at some point with the equally un-
hilarious message, 'Came here, but couldn't find
your house', so don't think about doing that
either.

  As a related point, it is also considered bad
form when talking to citizens of the Polish
capital, when they say 'Warsaw', to respond with
'What, the medium-sized industrial town in the
English Black Country?' It's not so much that
this is unfunny and annoying, just that they
won't have a clue what you're talking about.
Paul Crooke, www.walsallwonderland.co.uk

It is possible that there are uglier towns in the world
than Walsall, but if so I do not know them: and I
consider myself better than averagely travelled. But

while Walsall undoubtedly exists, it is difficult to know where precisely it begins and ends, because it is in the middle of one of the largest and most depressing contiguous areas of urban devastation in the world, the Black Country of the English Midlands. There is nowhere in the world where it is possible to travel such long distances without seeing anything grateful to the eye. To the hideousness of nineteenth-century industrialization is added the desolation of twentieth-century obsolescence. The Black Country looks like Ceausescu's Romania with fast food outlets.

Theodore Dalrymple, *The New Criterion*, September 2000

Walthamstow

In the early 20th-century the place became known as 'The Shoot' (as in rubbish shoot).

Watford

'The binge-drinking capital of Hertfordshire'

… according to the *Watford Observer* (30 October 2005). Writing of the town's 'sad, shabby, featureless' high street in 2006, a journalist in the same paper commented:

I sometimes wonder if Watford has been entered into some sort of contest to create the ugliest town in Britain.

A place just invented for people to catch connecting trains.

Sue George, *Guardian*, 4 February 2006

Elton John decided he wanted to rename Watford. He wanted to call it Queen of the South.

Tommy Docherty

Wembley

If Stratford is London's right armpit, Wembley is the left.

Tom Dyckhoff, *Observer*, 13 August 2005

Weston-super-Mare

'This God-forsaken hell-hole of a resort'

according to Bill Bryson. He elaborates:

The way I see it, there are three reasons never to be unhappy. First you were born ... Second, you are alive ... Third, you have plenty to eat, you live in a time of peace and 'Tie a Yellow Ribbon Round the Old Oak Tree' will never be number one again. If you bear these things in mind, you will never be truly unhappy – though in fairness I must point out that if you find yourself alone in Weston-super-Mare on a rainy Tuesday evening you may come close.

Bill Bryson, *Notes from a Small Island* (1995)

Wick

Wick ... the meanest of men's towns, set on what is surely the baldest of God's bays.
Robert Louis Stevenson, letter to his mother, 1868

Widnes

'So unloved by so many'

Widnes, the Cheshire chemical town so unloved by so many that Paul Simon famously wrote 'Homeward Bound' as he waited for the train out of it, would not be described by many outsiders as 'fantastic'.
www.sport.guardian.co.uk

Wigan

'The arse end of the world'

So called by Sue Nelson, when addressing an urban

regeneration conference in London in October 2004.
She began her speech thus:
**I should like to start by saying that Wigan is the arse
end of the world. London is the financial capital –
Wigan is the pie capital.**

Ms Nelson, the assistant chief executive of Keep
Britain Tidy (which is based in Wigan), went on to
talk about 'the two hubs of employment in Wigan –
JJB Sports and the Heinz Alphabetti factory'. Though
obliged to apologize for her remarks, the inhabitants
of Wigan still fumed:

**I think it's disgusting to say that. I love living here.
There must be worse places in the world. [Must
there? Ed.]**
Angela Schofield, 30, quoted in *Manchester News*,
14 October 2004

**There is nothing wrong with Wigan's pie reputation.
[Isn't there? See below. Ed.]**
Maurice Lindsay, chairman of Wigan's rugby league
club, quoted in the same publication

Meanwhile, the *Mirror*, punning on Wigan's most famous landmark (see below), headlined its report (14 October 2004) on the hoo-ha thus:

WIGAN REAR

> ## *Why Pies?*
>
> The people of Wigan are known as Pie-Eaters, not because of their love of pies, but because in 1926 the Wigan miners abandoned their strike sooner than their comrades in the rest of the country – and so 'ate humble pie'.
>
> *Just a town full of Pieheads*
> *Town full of Pieheads*
> *You're just a town full of Pieheads.*
> Chant sung by fans of Oldham Athletic

If Wigan is not the arse end of the world, why else did George Orwell pick on it as the epitome of poverty-struck frightfulness? In immortalizing the place he described it thus:

Labyrinths of little brick houses blackened by smoke, festering in planless chaos round miry alleys and little cindered yards where there are stinking dustbins and lines of grimy washing and half-ruinous w.c.'s.
George Orwell, *The Road to Wigan Pier* (1937)

Why Wigan Pier?

Wigan Pier, an area of Wigan on the Leeds–Liverpool Canal, takes its ironic name from the remains of a gantry, now little more than a few iron girders, protruding from a wall. The story goes that when a trainload of miners was delayed in Wigan next to the gantry, a miner asked a local where they were. The facetious reply came: 'Wigan Pier'.

The Wigan Alps, an area of old slag heaps, is an equally ironic coinage.

Wiltshire

Witless Wiltshire

In the past, natives of Wiltshire were often called 'Moonrakers', with an underlying implication of learning difficulties. The story goes that some Wiltshire rustics, having seen the moon's reflection in a pond, were observed trying to fish it out with a rake, suggesting some deficiency in the IQ department.

John Ayto and Ian Crofton, *Brewer's Britain and Ireland* (2005)

Windsor

Oh, my name is Diamond Lily,
I'm a whore in Piccadilly,
And my father has a brothel in the Strand,
My brother sells his arsehole
To the Guards at Windsor Castle,
We're the finest fucking family in the land.

Anon., 'Diamond Lily'

Woking

Doomed to destruction

I completely wreck and sack Woking – killing my neighbours in painful and eccentric ways …
H.G. Wells confides in a letter his plan for *The War of the Worlds* (1898), in which the Martians first land near Woking.

There are some places which have always been dreadful … Woking … is one of them.
Bill Murphy, *Home Truths* (2000)

Wolverhampton

Bus stop in Aston,
You're just a bus stop in Aston.
Chant favoured by other Birmingham fans, sung to the tune of 'Guantanamera'

Perhaps Wolverhampton's greatest claim to fame is

that it is home to England's first set of automatic traffic lights, erected in Princes Square in 1927.

Yorkshire

'I am in hell'

A huddle of cows are gloating in front of me. A gaggle of chickens is shrieking with laughter behind me. I am in hell. I am in a place called Yorkshire.
Johann Hari, *Independent*, 1 October 2004

Lovely scenery, but there are people in the West Riding who have lived there since 1106 but are still not accepted as true Yorkshiremen because rumour has it that their mother bought clogs from a pedlar who had a cousin in Prestbury, thereby blighting the bloodline forever. They make Londoners look like Hawaiian greeter girls.
Lucy Mangan, *Guardian*, 5 May 2006

Shake a bridle over a Yorkshireman's grave and he will rise and steal a horse.
Lancashire saying

Never … ask a Yorkshire farmer any question that can't be answered with 'a pint of Tetley's'.
Bill Bryson, *Notes from a Small Island* (1995)

My living in Yorkshire was so far out of the way, that it was actually twelve miles from a lemon.
Revd Sydney Smith

Yorkshire is definitely the county where men are men, and often have revolting wobbly beer guts to show for it.
Janet Street-Porter, quoted in the *Observer*, 7 August 2005

Regarding Yorkshire's claim to be the home of Robin Hood:
As Robin Hood wore bright green clothes, had a band of merry, not gruff, men and gave his money away, there is no way he could have hailed from

DON'T GO THERE!

Yorkshire.
Steve Little, letter to the *Guardian* (24 January 2004)

On your Yorkshire farms,
You pester the lambs when you hide in the grass,
You'd rather shag sheep than a fit normal lass,
On your Yorkshire farms …
Chant sung by Manchester United fans to Leeds fans,
to the tune of 'In My Liverpool Home'

You can shove your Yorkshire puddings up your arse,
You can shove your Yorkshire puddings up your arse,
You can shove your Yorkshire puddings,
Shove your Yorkshire puddings,
Shove your Yorkshire puddings up your arse –
SIDEWAYS!!!!
Chant sung by supporters of Macclesfield Town FC